The

AMERICAN
MAIL-ORDER
GOURMET

The

AMERICAN
MAIL-ORDER
GOURMET

The catalog of hundreds of hard-to-find delectable delights

NAOMI BLACK & MARK SMITH

A RUNNING PRESS/QUARTO BOOK

RUNNING PRESS BOOK PUBLISHERS
PHILADELPHIA, PENNSYLVANIA

A RUNNING PRESS/QUARTO BOOK
Copyright © 1986 by Quarto Marketing Ltd.

9 8 7 6 5 4 3 2 1

Digit on the right indicates the number of this printing.

Library of Congress Cataloging-in-Publication Data

Black, Naomi, 1957–
The American mail-order gourmet.

1. Food—United States—Catalogs.   I. Smith,
Mark, 1957–   II. Title.
TX354.5.B57   1986   641'.029'473   86-10032

ISBN: (cloth) 0-89471-388-4
(paper) 0-89471-389-2

THE AMERICAN MAIL—ORDER GOURMET
was prepared and produced by
Quarto Marketing Ltd.
15 West 26th Street
New York, N.Y. 10010

Editor: Pamela Hoenig
Art Director: Mary Moriarty
Photo Research: Susan M. Duane
Production Manager: Karen L. Greenberg
Designer: Liz Trovato

Typeset by BPE Graphics, Inc.
Color separations by South Seas Graphic Art Company Ltd.
Printed and bound in Hong Kong by Leefung-Asco Printers Ltd.

This book may be ordered from the publisher.
Please include $1.00 postage.
(But try your bookstore first.)

All prices of items listed in this catalog are subject to change.

Running Press Book Publishers
125 South 22nd Street
Philadelphia, Pennsylvania 19103

Acknowledgments

Many thanks go to all the manufacturers and distributors who took the time to fill out our questionnaires or talk to us or both. A warm acknowledgment also goes to Karla Olson and Felecia Abbadessa.

To Anne and John

CONTENTS

Foreword

The American Mail-Order Gourmet grew out of our curiosity at watching food trends come and go. With every passing of "the latest," we knew we could find at least one survivor, one food that was destined to become an old standby—if it wasn't one already. We searched for these, as well as for the good foods across the United States and Canada that stand up to generations of taste buds.

Our selection reflects our personal view of the mail-order market. We started out attending the NASFT Fancy Foods Show in Washington in 1984. There we gathered the names and addresses that eventually became the backbone of our master list. Friends, family, friends' families all helped us with their hometown or childhood recommendations. And we must nod our heads to Allison Engel and Margaret Engel, whose wonderful book *Food Finds* is another, more down-home celebration of American foods.

So, what you'll find within these pages offers a smorgasbord of cheeses, meats, jams, special sauces, fruitcakes, oils and vinegars, spices, nuts, and much more. To facilitate packing in as much information as we could into our write-ups, we developed a simple system that keys in convenience, credit card, and shipping information.

CON = *Conveniences.*
D = *Department stores. The product or products are available at selected department stores and gourmet shops.*
G = *Gift packages or assortments.*
H = *Holiday deadline.*
P = *Refund policy. The company offers some sort of refund or exchange if you receive damaged goods.*
R = *Recipes. Recipes or serving suggestions are included free of charge with the product(s).*
CC = *Credit cards.* The minimum you must spend to use the credit card is denoted in the parenthesis following credit card information.
AE = *American Express.*

CB = *Carte Blanche.*
DC = *Diners Club.*
MC = *MasterCard.*
V = *Visa.*
SH = *Shipping information.*
US = *United States (contiguous states).*
A&H = *Alaska and Hawaii.*
C = *Canada.*
UPS = *United Parcel Service.*
R = *Regular mail.*
X = *Express mail.*
The terms *regular mail* and *express mail* can be and are meant to be somewhat ambiguous, because each category includes more than one method by which ordered items can be sent.

When you're ordering through the mail, you should keep in mind a few things.
• Always make sure you include a street address for items that will be shipped UPS.
• Call first if you have any question about current shipping practices or prices.
• Write for the company's order forms if you're paying by credit card.

Please send us information about good foods we haven't included. We welcome all suggestions.

Naomi Black
c/o Quarto Marketing
15 West 26th St., 8th floor
New York, NY 10010

WHEELER PICTURES

CHAPTER ONE

Jams, Preserves and Honeys

American Spoon Foods

411 East Lake Street, Petoskey, Michigan 49770
616·347·9030

*M*ix the culinary ingenuity of one of America's finest chefs with the savvy of a native Michigan berrypicker/businessman and oodles of freshly handpicked wild berries from the hinterlands of northern Michigan and what you get are the fantastic berry preserves of American Spoon Foods—beyond doubt some of the best, most interesting preserves in the country. Native Michiganer Justin Rashid started the company in 1979 with the help of his friend, chef Lawrence Forgione, owner of An American Place in New York City and a pioneer of The New American Cuisine.

The creative partnership is ripe with fresh ideas on how to apply the new cuisine techniques to traditional American foods like wild handpicked berries. One of their most recent combinations is a preserve made from tayberries—a new berry hybrid of the loganberry and red raspberry. At once tangy, bright, and sweet, Tayberry Preserves are, in a word, extraordinary. A pack of two ten-ounce jars goes for $17.50 delivered.

Another delicious new American Spoon Foods product is Dried Tart Cherries from Traverse City, Michigan, "Cherry Capitol of the World." These flavorful morsels are the perfect hiker's snack—or you can add them to muffins, breads, and cookies for a tangy accent. A two-pound bag with recipes costs $17.50.

Conveniences: G, R, P **Credit Cards:** MC, V, ($10.00) **Shipping:** U.S.—R, UPS

American Spoon Foods

Bainbridge's Festive Foods

P.O. Box 15805, Nashville, Tennessee 37215

615·383·5157

This family-owned company out of Nashville, Tennessee, produces a large and interesting variety of unusual sweet and savory jellies, each one with an unmistakably singular character. In the sweet category, there is a Black Walnut Jelly, Apple Pie Jelly, Cranberry Pineapple Jelly, Fig Berry Preserves (minced fine and jellylike), Lemon Honey, Blackberry, Fancy Red Raspberry, Cherry Pie Jelly, and Spiced Plum. Savory jellies include Golden Kiwi Mint, Garlic with Parsley, Spring Onion, and three delicious pepper jellies—one hot, a mild green, and a mild red. But Bainbridge's hasn't chiseled out the categories in stone. In fact, many of the "sweet" jellies go hand-in-glove with meat, fish, poultry, and vegetable dishes, and recipes are included with each order to show you how.

Bainbridge's jellies come in ten-ounce jars at $3.75 a jar, with a four-jar minimum order. Gift boxes of four-jar assortments are also available; just pick your favorite four flavors.

Conveniences: G, H, D, P, R **Credit Cards:** MC, V **Shipping:** U.S.—UPS; A&H—UPS; C—UPS

Bainbridge's Festive Foods

Cascade Conserves

P.O. Box 8306, Portland, Oregon 97207

503·224·6366

*W*e've tasted a lot of jams, preserves, and jellies in our time, and Cascade Conserves' Seedless Marionberry Conserve is one of the best. It's a fine wine of the berry world, rich and flavorful without being overly tart or sweet.
Cascade Conserves is one of a handful of small, high-quality, Northwest companies that use the exceptional berries from the region to produce heavenly conserves. There are regularly stocked varieties—Marionberry, Orange Marmalade, Strawberry, Red Raspberry, Seedless Red Raspberry, and Blueberry—in addition to limited-production varieties, such as Wild Mountain Blackberry, the berry of which is found in patches that change annually. Don't mistake these gems with the more abundant Evergreen and Himalaya blackberries; both of these are also special—to bears as well as humans so the availability varies.
The fall 1985 offerings included Boysenberry, Loganberry, Cascadeberry, Gooseberry, and Huckleberry. All are available in 1.5-ounce and twelve-ounce jars for $1.25 and $4.50, respectively, plus a $1.50 shipping charge for all orders under $15.00. The package design—a simple label on a plain jar, tied with a thin burgundy cloth ribbon—makes these excellent presents for any time of the year. (Be sure to ask for the ribbon.) Gift boxes of four small jars can be packed with your choice of flavors in wood excelsior in an old-fashioned berry halleck, shrink-wrapped and ribboned. Or you may choose two of the larger jars to be packed in a rustic vine basket. Both can be wrapped in Cascade Conserves' tasteful burgundy paper and ribbon, at your request ($1.75 extra). A gift card with your message will be included gratis. If you're shopping in the Pacific Northwest, New York City, or California, you can stop in for the conserves at Made in Oregon Stores; or at Rex's Markets and Delicatessens and Pike Place Market (Seattle); The Irvine Ranch Farmer's Markets, Beverly Center, and Fashion Island of Newport Beach (California); and Balducci's (New York).

Conveniences: D ,G ,P **Credit Cards:** MC, V **Shipping:** U.S.—UPS (unless otherwise requested); A&H—R, X, UPS; C—R, X, UPS

Clearbrook Farms

5514 Fair Lane, Fairfax, Ohio 45227

513·271·2053

*C*incinnati's Cohen family jarred and gave their special fruit preserves as holiday gifts for twenty-seven years before they considered selling them. "My father thought the compliments and then demands for the preserves year-round were just polite thank-yous," explains Dan Cohen, vice-president of sales for Clearbrook Farms. The company now sells 25,000 cases each year, and numbers are growing. High quality combined with an extraordinary variety of fruit preserves from around the country seems to be Clearbrook's formula for success.
"We buy only the best fruit from the best growing regions in the United States: damson plums from Michigan, wild blueberries from Maine, red and black raspberries from Oregon, just to name a few," Cohen says. "Then we show the source on our label, so people know what they're getting."
Other flavors include Bittersweet Orange Marmalade, California Peach, Apricot and Apricot-Pineapple, Oregon Marion Blackberry and Boysenberry, Michigan Strawberry, Red Tart Cherry and Black Cherry, and Concord Grape. All preserve flavors come in twenty-four-ounce French canning jars that are gift-packed in handsome slatted-wood crates. One jar is $13.50, two are $21.00. Three thirteen-ounce jars of preserves in a slatted crate are $16.50. Or, if you're buying for yourself and can do without the wood crate, a single jar is $11.50.

Conveniences: G, H, D, R **Credit Cards:** none **Shipping:** U.S.—UPS; A&H—UPS; C—UPS

House of Webster

Box 488, 1013 North Second Street, Rogers, Arkansas 72757

501·636·4640

*T*he House of Webster has specialized in homemade country-style food gifts since 1934 and has gained an unshakable reputation for high quality. Roy Webster, founder and owner of House of Webster, chalks up his company's success to the system of free enterprise, and, if you stop by his place next time you're down in Rogers, Arkansas, he'll be happy to tell you why.

The gift pack pictured here is a good example of the Webster line. It contains six eleven-ounce jars of homemade preserves and jellies (Peach, Strawberry, and Cherry preserves; and Crab Apple, Concord Grape, and Santa Rosa Plum jellies), a two-and-one-half-pound slab of country-cured and hickory-smoked bacon, and three one-pound bags of Webster's Flaky Buttermilk Biscuit Mix. The package comes in an attractive illustrated gift box for $23.75, plus shipping. House of Webster has a multitude of other gift combinations. For a catalog, write to the above address to the attention of Roy.

Conveniences: G, P, H **Credit Cards:** none **Shipping:** U.S.—R, X, UPS; A&H—R, X; C—R, X

Clearbrook Farms

CLEARBROOK FARMS

Black-Eyed Susans

½ cup solid shortening
¾ cup firmly-packed light brown sugar
1 egg
1 teaspoon vanilla extract
¾ cup flour
½ teaspoon salt
1¼ cups rolled oats
1¾ cups shredded coconut
Clearbrook Farms Preserves

In a large mixing bowl, cream together shortening and sugar. Add egg and vanilla and beat well. Gradually sift in the flour and salt and blend thoroughly. Add oats and ¾ cup of the coconut and mix well. Cover and refrigerate until well chilled.

Preheat oven to 300°F.

Shape the chilled dough into balls about 1-inch in diameter. Roll balls in the remaining coconut and place on greased cookie sheets. Make a thumbprint in the top of each ball and fill dents with your favorite Clearbrook Farms Preserves. Bake in the center of the oven for 25 to 30 minutes, or until lightly browned.

Makes about 36 cookies.

TONY CENICOLA

Maury Island Farming Company

Moon Shine Trading Company

House of Webster

Maury Island Farming Company

Route 3   Box 238, Vashon, Washington 98070

206·463·5617

*P*eter and Jude Shepard are "dedicated to bringing the full flavors of classic Pacific Northwest berries to berry lovers everywhere." They begin by using more fruit than sugar, by weight, in their jams and jellies, choosing the finest fruits from the area. They even grow their own currants for their Red Currant Jelly and the newer, sweeter Raspberry-Currant Preserves. Made in small batches, the preserves come in a rainbow of flavors: Blackberry Jelly, Blueberry Jelly and Jam, Red Raspberry Jam and Jelly, Strawberry Preserves, Bittersweet Orange and Lemon Marmalade. The 60 percent fruit toppings are also quite good; more pourable than jams, they are perfect for parfaits and are equally yummy on waffles, blintzes, or chocolate tortes.

A two-jar (ten-ounces each) order, the minimum, is $10.50 postpaid, but you should probably opt for the assorted sample-pack of four five-and-one-half-ounce jars ($13.50), or the three-pack of ten-ounce jars ($15.95). You can make the selection yourself or leave it up to the Shepards, who also will be happy to enclose a note with the gift—either one you have sent them or instructed them to write. Get your orders in by December 10 at the latest to beat the holiday deadline. The company's unpretentious catalog also offers truly "delicious and interesting things for the holidays from the Puget Sound Country." Besides smoked fish, and sugar-free apple butters, these include a fresh holly wreath and shredded grape-vine wood for barbecuing.

Conveniences: G, H, P **Credit Cards:** MC, V **Shipping:** U.S.—UPS; A&H—R, X, UPS; C—R, X, UPS

Moon Shine Trading Company

P.O. Box 896, Winters, California 95694

916·795·2092

*T*he Gourmet Honey Collection®—the brainchild of a California duo operating out of Winters, a small town in the fertile foothills of the Coastal Mountains—is the cornerstone of this couple's dream of increasing honey consumption in North America, especially the United States. With a look at and a taste of their honeys, you'd be hard-pressed not to admit that they'll accomplish their goal. Just the names are evocative of rich, meltingly smooth dreams on the tongue: Hawaiian Creamy Lehua (a spicy white honey that's good for spreading), California Eucalyptus Honey (a deep-scented, mineral-rich mild variety), High Plains Sweet Clover (a light honey with a characteristic essence of cinnamon). The California Black Button Sage, known for its water-white color and light flavor, complements the butterscotchy Hawaiian Christmas Berry. With choices like these, you'll opt for more than one jar of honey on your shelf. Other varieties include the sweet, delicate California Yellow Star Thistle; the hearty California Sunflower, which lends itself particularly well to baking; Florida White Tupelo, a distinctive nongranulating honey; Creamy Desert Garden, a creamy white honey whose predominant floral sources are the mesquite, catclaw, and prickly pear cacti. Last but not least is the California Orange Blossom, the standard by which most honeys are judged, a superior sweet specialty.

Both one-pound ($3.50 and up) and two-and-a-half-ounce ($1.75 to $2.50) jars are available. Lovers of comb honey may order High Plains Sweet Clover and Rocky Mountain Wildflower varieties in eight-ounce containers. And there's a Santa Bear for Christmas giving, as well as a few gift packages. Holiday orders should be in by November 15. There's a $20.00 minimum, but the order can be mixed. Shipping costs depend on the destination.

Conveniences: D, G, H, P, R (in gift boxes) **Credit Cards:** none **Shipping:** U.S.—UPS; A&H—R, UPS; C—R

My Grandmama's, Inc.

P.O. Box 1115, Deerfield Beach, Florida 33441

305·421·4312

Open the gold-foil box, and the top flap reveals a finely scripted "Love is Eternal." The real treasure lies tucked inside. My Grandmama's Love Apple Jam is a lovingly made recreation of an old Pennsylvania recipe. Made with tomatoes, which were once "believed to possess aphrodisiac properties, and were therefore feared by virtuous maidens," this jam makes a predominantly sweet but somewhat tart impression on the tongue. It's a perfect complement to morning muffins or evening hors d'oeuvre.

My Grandmama's also makes a delicious Wild Orange Jam and Hot Pepper Jelly. All come with the message to "spread a little love," Pat Hayes Kinkaid's personal touch. The one-pound jars sell for $7.50 each, and the company will gladly mail gifts with an enclosed card directly to your chosen recipient. Shipping charges are added only to those destinations outside the contiguous U.S.

Conveniences: D, G, P **Credit Cards:** MC, V **Shipping:** U.S.—UPS; A&H—R; C—R

Napa Valley Connection

1201 Main Street, St. Helena, California 94574

707·963·1111 or 1·800·422·1111

Based in the quaint burg of St. Helena, in the heart of California's prime wine country, this young company is certainly in the right position for choosing the best lots of wine from which to make their fantastic jellies.

Napa Valley Connection produces only two wine jellies—Cabernet Sauvignon and Sauvignon Blanc—but they are of such great character and depth, it seems the possibilities are well-covered. You can find the jellies at Macy's, Harris, and Neiman-Marcus, or you can order them through the catalogs of Neiman-Marcus, Marriot Hotels, and Napa Valley Connection itself. (Also note their toll-free number.) The jellies come in three jar sizes—two-and-a-half ounce, seven-ounce, and five pound, and are quite reasonably priced.

Conveniences: H, D, R **Credit Cards:** AE, MC, V ($15.00) **Shipping:** U.S.—R, UPS; A&H—R, X

Napa Valley Connection

Sarabeth's Kitchen

My Grandmama's, Inc.

Sarabeth's Kitchen

423 Amsterdam Avenue, New York, New York 10024

212·496·6280

*W*hen you order Sarabeth's sweet things, you are getting a taste of New York, a taste of what people patiently wait—sometimes for hours—to sample in Sarabeth's cafés. Granted, they're also thinking of Sarabeth's pumpkin muffins and cream scones as they wait, *but* it's her jams and butters that tourists and regulars alike walk out with: the classic Sarabeth Orange-Apricot Marmalade; the Plum Loco combination of plums, apples, and lemons; Apricadabra, a "bewitching" blend of apricots, pineapple, and currants ("an apricot-lover's dream"); Miss Figgy preserves; and a Lemon-Pear Butter that *New York* magazine's Barbara Costikyan wrote was "so dulcet you can eat it neat from the jar." And there's more. We've seen a patron buy one jar of Chunky Apple Butter and open it amid her friends; within seconds, her three comrades were in line for their own fruit spreads.

With no additives or preservatives—just fruit and sugar—these preserves are made from hand-cut fruits that offer a unique texture in the vast world of store preserves. These are standouts. Without question.

Others in the Sarabeth line include: Peach-Apricot Preserve; Fruit Fantasy; Cranberry Relish (available November through January); and Rosy Cheeks, an "artful marriage of strawberry and apple" (available April through August). The Fruit Fantasy is an unusual item on the list. The delectable peaches-raisins-and-almond combo is a chewy dream, a perfect match for the freshest plain yogurt you can find. Or add it to turkey stuffing, rest it beside sweet potato pie or ham, or use it to top off a scoop or two of ice cream.

No mention of Sarabeth can be complete without a whisper about Beau Pear. Heart-shaped and lovingly poached, the pears are an October-through-February creation designed to melt—or warm—others' hearts.

All but Beau Pear can be gift-boxed in a three-jar (sixteen ounces each) package for $31.00, including shipping and handling. Beau Pear is available gift-boxed for $18.50 for each sixteen-ounce jar. Send your Thanksgiving and Christmas orders in a month before the holiday. Sarabeth's cooking can also be found at major department stores such as Bloomingdale's, Macy's, Rich's, and Neiman-Marcus.

Conveniences: D, G, H, P **Credit Cards:** AE ($15), MC ($25), V ($25) **Shipping:** U.S.—UPS; A&H—UPS; C—R, UPS (Toronto)

Vermont's Clearview Farms, Inc.

RR #1, Enosburg Falls, Vermont 05450

802·933·2537

*W*orking from the original recipes of "Gram," whom we assume to be a specific great-grandmother cook in the old American tradition, this small Vermont company has brought farm-style relish-making well into the realm of art. Probably their most universal relish is one called Old Fashioned Piccalilli, which is a combination of cabbage, green tomatoes, red and green peppers, onions, spices, herbs, brown sugar, and vinegar. What a sweet, tangy beauty! Use it on or with any number of savory dishes—meats, vegetables, cheeses, hors d'oeuvre, and others—for a fresh and lively taste accent. Farmstead Zucchini Relish is another of Clearview Farms' more traditional concoctions. It, too, is a unique and delicious treat. But read on for some of their more innovative relish creations: First, there's Honied Carrot Relish, a blend of julienned carrots, grated onions, and whole raisins simmered in honey, vinegar, and spices. Next, what they call their Rembrandt of Relishes, is Cranberry Orange Relish, made with 100-percent-pure Vermont Maple syrup and bursting with a snappy rainbow of farm-fresh flavors.

All Vermont Clearview Farms relishes come in eight-ounce jars. The Piccalilli and Zucchini Relish sell for $2.49, the Honied Carrot Relish is $2.89, and the Cranberry Orange Relish is $3.09. Shipping charges depend on destination.

Conveniences: H, P, R **Credit Cards:** MC, V **Shipping:** U.S.—UPS; A&H—UPS; C—UPS

Vermont's Clearview Farms, Inc.

SANDRA DOSPASSOS

CHAPTER TWO

Sweet and Savory Sauces and Relishes

Beaverton Foods

4220 SW Cedar Hills Boulevard, Beaverton, Oregon 97005

503·643·7634

*B*eaverton Foods has been a grower, processor, and packer of quality specialty mustards, horseradishes, and sauces since 1925. In their time, they have developed an astounding array of products. They now offer roughly eighteen different mustards, including such unusual and delicious ones as Hickory Smoke Mustard, Madagascar Green Peppercorn Mustard, Stone Ground Cheese Mustard, and Beef Log Mustard. Their ethnic-style mustards include Olde English Hot, Russian Hot, Dusseldorf Hot, Chinese Hot, Hawaiian Pineapple, Wurstmeister Sausage, Bavarian Beer, and more. What Beaverton has done with mustards, they also have done with horseradish. Their variety includes 100-percent-pure Instant Horseradish, plain Kosher Style—with and without beets—Whipped Horseradish, Olde English, Cream Style, and others.

Beaverton Foods markets their products under three different brand names: Old Spice, Beaver, and Inglehoffer. Only Old Spice and Beaver brands offer all the above variations. They come in gift packs of six four-ounce jars for $6.95, or by the twelve-jar case for $12.00. If you're thinking of a gift, choose Inglehoffer brand, which is attractively packaged in German-style jars and a handsome wood crate.

Conveniences: G, P **Credit Cards:** AE, MC, V **Shipping:** U.S.—R, X, UPS; A&H—R, UPS; C—R

Beaverton Foods

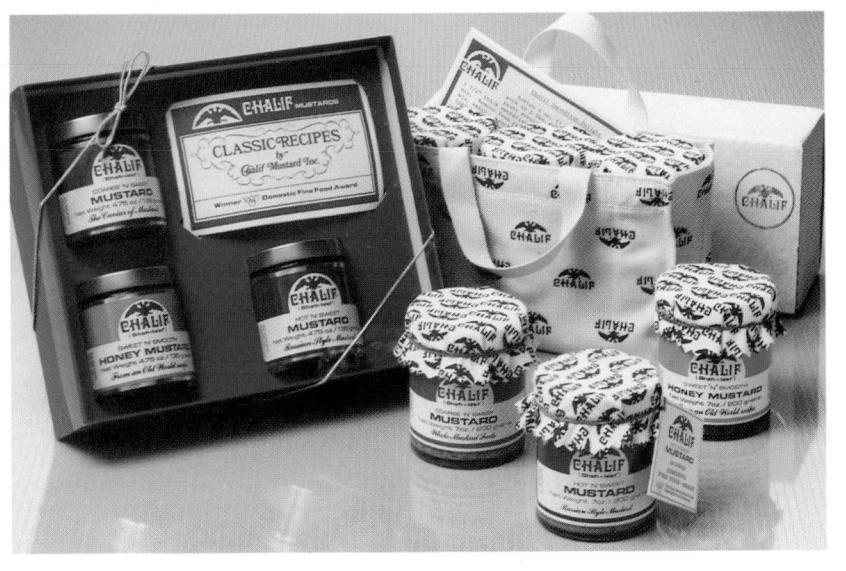

Chalif, Inc.

Chalif, Inc.

P.O. Box 27220, Wyndmoor, Pennsylvania 19118

215·233·2023

*T*he story of this company's phenomenal success in the specialty food industry has become an inspiration and a model for many small gourmet food companies in America. In 1982, Liz and Nick Thomas were out of work and worried about mounting bills and tuitions for their four children. They invested their last two hundred dollars to produce the first batch of Chalif Hot 'n' Sweet Mustard, using an old family recipe. The following year their smooth, dark, and rich product won the NASFT Domestic Fine Food Award, certainly one of the most prestigious honors in the industry, and the Thomases were suddenly shuffling down Success Street.

Today, Chalif makes two other gourmet mustards—Coarse 'n' Sassy, a sensual blend of whole mustard seeds and horseradish, and Sweet 'n' Smooth Honey Mustard. In 1985, Chalif introduced Chalif Stirling Sauce—a zesty marinade for steak, fish, and poultry that contains finely ground peaches and cashew nuts—as well as a new line of premium flavored mayonnaises called Mayonnaise Alexandra. Flavors include Strawberries & Champagne, Mustard Seed Dill, Basil, Mint Sesame, and Curry Tarragon. They come in eight-ounce jars at $2.50 a jar, with a five-jar minimum. Stirling Sauce comes in a twelve-ounce bottle for $5.00, shipping included, and Chalif Mustards come in seven-ounce jars at $3.50 a jar, three-jar minimum. Gift-box mustard assortments contain three 4.75-ounce jars and a "Classic Chalif Recipes" booklet for $12.00.

Conveniences: G, H, R, P **Credit Cards:** none **Shipping:** U.S.—UPS; A&H—R, UPS; C—R, UPS

Conner Farms Inc.

P.O. Box 1566, Dalton, Georgia 30722-1566

404·226·5674

*T*he yellow granex type F hybrid onion is a very fine onion by any standard. But only when it is grown under the gentle climatic conditions of south Georgia and, furthermore, in the unique sandy soil within thirty-five miles of Vidalia, Georgia, does the granex type F become a Vidalia Onion—without question the sweetest, most succulent onion in the world. Conner Farms, a six-generation family farm just outside Vidalia, has grown onions for seventy-five years, but not until 1980 did an insightful member of the Conner clan by the name of Beverly Conner Cole fully realize the Vidalia onion's unique quality and marketing potential. Since then, Beverly has worked hard to get the word out about her region's specialty, with the result that the Vidalia Onion is now probably the world's most sought-after gourmet onion.

Conner Farms' Vidalia Onion Pickles and Relish won the NASFT Domestic Fine Food Award in 1982, for being "the most exciting, interesting, and exceptional food product, old or new" for that year. Due to the limited supply of Vidalia Onions, you must order quickly. One sixteen-ounce jar of either the pickles or relish sells for $5.75. Ms. Conner Cole has developed some other outstanding uses for Vidalias, such as her Vidalia Sweet Onion Mustard, which is $4.75 for nine ounces, and Vidalia Onion Salad Dressing, sixteen ounces for $5.50.

Conner Farms grows other vegetables, and Beverly has put them to good use, too. At the NASFT show in Atlanta in 1985, her Jezebel Sauce (a southern-style horseradish fruit mustard) and her Blocker's Barbecue Sauce won "Best of Aisle" awards. The Jezebel Sauce is nine ounces for $3.95, and Blocker's Barbecue is sixteen ounces for $4.95.

Conveniences: G, R, P, H **Credit Cards:** MC, V **Shipping:** U.S.—UPS; A&H—R, UPS; C—R, UPS

Conner Farms Inc.

Groff's Farm Enterprises

Groff's Farm Enterprises

RD 3, Box 912, Mount Joy, Pennsylvania 17552

717·653·2048

"*I* think of Groff's Farm as a wonderful example of how great American food can be," wrote world-renowned food critic James Beard, in reference to the gourmet edibles produced by this family-run company out of Mount Joy, Pennsylvania. The Groff's Farm line of farm-fresh country relishes is truly one of the best, most original American relish selections in existence. Featuring sweet-and-sour relishes made in authentic Pennsylvania Dutch style, the line includes Pickled Celery, Corn Relish, Bread & Butter Pickles, a delectable mixture of vegetables they call Chow Chow, and Groff's famous Spiced Cantaloupe. All five relishes are delicious alone, in salads, or as hors d'oeuvre accents.

Betty Groff, originator of the relish line, grew up in a traditional Mennonite farm home and learned how to prepare the wonderful country dishes that reflect the bounty of the rolling farmlands of Lancaster County.

Groff's Farm Relishes are packaged in sixteen-ounce jars with attractive cloth-and-gold-string tops. They are available in a three-jar gift-pack selection at $7.00, plus shipping, and a six-jar gift pack for $13.50.

Conveniences: G, D **Credit Cards:** AE, MC, V **Shipping:** U.S.—UPS; A&H—UPS; C—UPS

Harmon's Gourmet Inc.

Harmon's Gourmet Inc.

4226 South Produce Plaza, Vernon, California 90058

213·589·1616

*B*efore 1973, Helen Harmon was happy at home in her kitchen, cooking and concocting her own variety of specialty eats. Her favorite was a mild green pepper jelly that added great flavor to beef and poultry. But Helen knew she was no gourmet. Or was she? When her friends and family tasted Helen's jelly, they crowned her chef, and with this boost of confidence behind her, Helen quickly sold forty-six cases of her jelly to Jurgensen's, California's fanciest grocery chain. Helen Harmon never looked back.

Harmon soon expanded her pepper jelly line to include two more unique variations: Hot-Hot Pepper Jelly, made with jalapeño peppers, and Tangy Red Pepper Jelly. Following that success, she has developed one of the most varied and unusual selections of flavored mustards anywhere. They include Toasted Onion, Horseradish, Jalapeño, Dill, Toasted Sesame, Sweet-Hot, Wheat Germ 'N Honey, Pepper-Hot, Teriyaki, and Champagne-Honey. Each is distinct and delicious.

Harmon's Gourmet offers gift packs in many combinations. The pepper jellies come in a three-pound Trio Gift Pack for $10.50. At the same price and weight comes the Mustard Trio, which includes the Sweet-Hot, Dill, and Toasted Onion. The Six-Pack Gift Box has the three pepper jellies and three mustards for $17.50.

Conveniences: G, P, R **Credit Cards:** none **Shipping:** U.S.—UPS; A&H—R; C—R

Jasmine & Bread

RR 2 Box 256, South Royalton, Vermont 05068

802·763·7115

For years, catsup has been the undisputed catchall condiment of the average American eater. Jasmine & Bread now takes you into a new condiment dimension with its "Beyond Catsup," an original, unique, and versatile gourmet blend of fresh tomatoes, apples, vegetables, and spices that beats ordinary catsup by a mile. It's great on hamburgers, hotdogs, and french fries but is also superb basted on broiled chicken, fish, pork, ribs, and beef.

Sherrie Maurer developed the recipe at home in the tiny burg of South Royalton, Vermont. At the urging of friends and her husband, Hugh, Sherrie started to market the concoction by making 350 jars in her own kitchen. That was in 1984. The following year she made five thousand jars, the stores ran out, and people demanded more. It seems once you go "Beyond Catsup," there's no turning back.

Beyond Catsup comes in a thirteen-ounce jar and sells for $3.98, plus $1.50 for shipping and handling. Jasmine & Bread has recently brought out another delicious original—"Beyond Belief," a tomato/pear combination with a spicy hint of chili peppers. A nine-ounce jar goes for $3.25, plus $1.50 for shipping and handling.

Conveniences: G **Credit Cards:** none **Shipping:** U.S.—UPS; A&H—UPS; C—UPS

The Larder of Lady Bustle, Limited

P.O. Box 53393, Atlanta, Georgia 30355

404·584·0525

The Larder of Lady Bustle brings to you The Original Lemon Jam—a delicacy from England and now from the Deep South. Lemon Jam is an old family recipe with an Old English quality. It is made in small batches of all natural ingredients with no preservatives.

The adaptability of Lemon Jam is as limited as your imagination. Use it as a jam in tarts or spread it on croissants, toast, or muffins. Try it as a dessert sauce on ice cream, pound cake, gingerbread, angel food cake, or lady fingers. It makes an excellent and delicious topping on cheesecake or glaze on chicken, and it's great straight, too.

An eight-ounce jar sells for $5.00.

This fine Atlanta company has recently come out with another unique and delightful product—Lord Bustle's Favourite Raisin Sauce. This is an extraordinary sweet-and-sour sauce made from a perfect blend of raisins, mustard, vinegar, sugar, eggs, and other natural ingredients. It's sensational with ham or mixed with sour cream as a dip.

An eight-ounce jar sells for $4.75.

For yet another unique experience from Lady Bustle's larder, try her Brandied Cranberries. They're equally excellent on turkey, hare, or ice cream. The eight-ounce jar is $5.50.

Conveniences: H, P, G **Credit Cards:** MC, V ($20.00) **Shipping:** U.S.—UPS; A&H—UPS; C—UPS

The Larder of Lady Bustle, Limited

Jasmine & Bread

Rowena's and Captain Jaap's

758 West 22nd Street, Norfolk, Virginia 23517

804·627·8699

*W*hen Captain Jaap's label states that his Special Steak & Hamburger Sauce is a "spicy sauce that is terrific on hamburger, steak, your favorite meatloaf, pork barbecue, or even white rice," it's very true. Whoever wrote the copy left off that it's the best dressing for turkey sandwiches we've ever tasted. The mustard, tomato paste, and seasonings combine with just the right tang; be prepared for a slight but very pleasant nip to the sauce, which sells for $4 and $6.50 for ten-ounce and eighteen-ounce jars, respectively.

The full line of Captain Jaap's products includes a Barbecue and Cooking Sauce, a Cranberry Nut Conserve that is only available in winter, an Oriental Sweet and Sour Sauce, a Virginia Hunt Sauce, Lemon Garlic Olive Oil, Old Fashioned Spiced Vinegar, and two new low-calorie, sodium-free tomato and vegetable-based blends—Galley Sauce and a more full-bodied Mariner's Sauce. Prices range between $4 and $6.50.

The complementary product line, Rowena's, brings jams and jellies to the fore. There's Sweet Basil Jelly, Carrot Jam, Lemon Curd, Orange Sauterne Jelly, Peach Orange Clove Jam, and Pepper Jelly—each $4 for eight to nine-and-a-half ounces. A tasty sweet-and-sour mustard also sells for $4 (nine ounces).

On request, the jars can be "gift wrapped" in a red-and-white polka dot cloth bag with a white bow to boot (add $1.50 for each bag). Gift baskets are also available; choose any two or four jams, jellies, or sauces for $12.50 or $21. The list doesn't stop there. You can opt for a dark red gift box or any of four picnic hampers. Write for details on these.

Conveniences: D, G, P, R **Credit Cards:** Choice, MC, V **Shipping:** U.S.—UPS; A&H—UPS; C—UPS

Rowena's and Captain Jaap's

*R*owena Jaap and her husband, Captain Joseph Jaap, have made a cozy home of their factory, where they produce a wonderful almond pound cake and over a dozen jams, jellies, and sauces that are now distributed to more than six hundred stores. The cannery's hominess comes from the numerous collectibles and souvenirs of the retired Navy captain: Japanese lamps, loveseats, brass candlesticks. Quilted tablecloths and a fireplace add to the charm. Visitors are always welcome, say the Jaaps.

"The cannery is really the American dream—to be on your own." For the Jaaps, the dream was creative cooking. Like many small businesses, this one developed from a mix of good products, a dash of serendipity, and lots of encouragement. A local school, close to its demise from lack of funds, bounced back with fifteen thousand dollars raised from a fair and bake sale that the Jaaps had helped organize. Rowena took heart from that experience and soon was selling her good foods in Norfolk, Virginia's, small shops.

The next step, the factory, emerged with the help of her husband, who contributed some of the recipes in addition to holding down the jobs of bookkeeper, stockboy, cook, and maintenance man.

The couple are well-suited to the business. She majored in biology and chemistry, he received a master's in business administration. And they both take pride in this shared venture, evidenced by their eponymic labels. Captain Jaap's has one look with its gold foil-topped squarish jars, while Rowena's sports another, with fabric and gold cord around the top of round, tall jars.

The Jaaps make the company what it is: a sound, substantial business with lots of good taste.

Mustard Sauce for Chicken, Veal, or Filet of Beef Melt 3 tablespoons butter in heavy skillet and sauté 2 chopped scallions. Lightly flour chicken, veal or beef and brown about 5 minutes on each side in skillet. Remove meat from skillet and add ¼ cup dry vermouth for chicken or veal or ¼ cup bourbon for beef. At this point, you may also add some sautéed mushrooms if you are cooking beef. Simmer gently, stir in ¼ cup Sweet & Sour Mustard and ½ cup heavy cream and boil until sauce is reduced. Pour sauce over your warm chicken, veal, or beef.

Pepper Jelly Stuffing Melt ½ cup butter. Add 1 cup (2 large stalks) chopped celery, 1 cup chopped onion and ½ cup chopped, fresh parsley or ¼ cup dried parsley. Cook until soft—about 5 minutes. Add one 8-ounce bag of herb-seasoned stuffing mix and then add 6-8 tablespoons Pepper Jelly. Please taste at this point. You may now wish to make dressing balls. Add 1 egg to dressing and mix. With your hands, press dressing tightly in the shape and size of a tennis ball or a little smaller. Bake at 400° for 5-10 minutes until edges are slightly brown. These are fun to serve and freeze very well.

Veal or Chicken Rolls For best results, these should be made ahead and chilled. Slice and serve at room temperature. Using veal or chicken, pound each piece till at least ¼-inch thick. Place 2-3 tablespoons Mariner's Sauce on each piece. Roll up, jellyroll fashion, not rolling too tightly. Brown rolls in nonstick pan (regular pan, use 1 tablespoon oil). Cover pan, lower heat, and allow to steam for 10-15 minutes. This is a lovely and elegant dish for company. Serve with extra sauce.

Rowena's and Captain Jaap's

Sterling Mountain Maple Inc.

Box 17, Waterville, Vermont 05492

802·644·2487

Sterling Mountain Maple has an angle: Owners Susan and Nicholas Wylie have incorporated their New York advertising and marketing experience into their second-career maple business in Waterville, Vermont, to produce some of the most imaginative maple syrup packaging ever. They put their purest Vermont Maple Syrup in handsome champagne-type bottles, with fancy vintnerlike labels and gold foil cork covers. At a glance, you'd think it was a bottle of fine French wine! A 25.4-ounce bottle is $12.95, plus $2.75 shipping.

Golden Maple Crystals—that delectable dessert enhancer of sweet lovers in the know—are another specialty of Sterling Mountain. Add them to your regular coffee or tea as a tasty substitute to sugar, sprinkle them on ice cream, cereal, strawberries, or even melt them in boiling water to make instant maple syrup. They come in an attractive gold twelve-ounce pouch for $13.59, plus $2.50 for shipping.

All Sterling Mountain Maple products have the coveted Vermont Seal of Quality and come gift-boxed with hand-drawn gift cards.

Conveniences: G, R, P, H, D **Credit Cards:** MC, V ($35.00) **Shipping:** U.S.—R, X, UPS

Sugar's Kitchen

7567 High Avenue, La Jolla, California 92037

619·456·1943

Sugar Birdsall of Tucson, Arizona, and La Jolla, California, has developed some winning combinations with her Arizona Champagne Sauces: piquant, full-bodied flavor, and no salt! Craig Claiborne of the *New York Times* called Sugar's treats "some of the most interesting no-salt food products to find their way into my refrigerator." Gene Benton of *Bon Appetit* magazine went further. He called Ms. Birdsall's Arizona Champagne Mustard Sauce "one of the best homemade specialty mustards I've tasted in years."

There are three now-famous Arizona Champagne Mustard Sauces: Hot, Cajun Style, and Regular. They're great on cold cuts, cheeses, and sandwiches, but also do wonders when spread on fish, chicken, roasts, or ham before cooking. In Birdsall's same sauce family is a wonderful Vegetables Dip that's great with crackers, chips, cheeses, and raw vegetables. Sugar Birdsall also makes a dry Arizona Southwest Mix, which you can add to crushed tomatoes and green chilis for a fresh salsa, or use in soups, stews, or omelets, and a dry Arizona Herbal Spice Dip Mix for making dips. Both are sugar- and salt-free.

All Arizona Champagne Sauces and Mixes come in eight-ounce jars gift-boxed in combinations of your choice. A box of any three jars is $12.75; four jars are $15.85; six jars are $23.00. They are also available in sixteen-ounce jars, any two for $13.75.

Conveniences: G, R, P, H **Credit Cards:** none **Shipping:** U.S.—UPS; A&H—UPS; C—UPS

Sterling Mountain Maple Inc.

Sugar's Kitchen

WHEELER PICTURES

CHAPTER THREE

Dessert Sauces

Dearborn

1 Christopher Street, New York, New York 10014
212·691·9153

*D*earborn's Chocolate Truffle Kit is a marvelous introduction to the wonderful world of chocolate truffles. Everything you need is included—a thirteen-ounce jar of Dearborn's Chocolate Sauce, a tin of fine cocoa powder, a forming spoon and candy papers, and Dearborn's truffle recipe book, which offers several delightful variations on Dearborn's proven truffle theme. A perfect gift for confirmed chocoholics and a marvel for truffle-making neophytes, the kit sells for $16.00, plus $3.50 shipping.

This small four-year-old company also features a line of excellent dessert sauces and three fancy cocktail nut combinations. The sauces include a Butterscotch Sauce (great over baked apples), a Maple Sauce (baste a roast chicken with it!), a Chocolate Sauce (so thick you can ice a cake with it), and a White Chocolate & Hazelnut Sauce (ideal as a frosting for carrot cake). Each thirteen-ounce jar goes for $10.50, shipping included, or a boxed Trio Gift Set (your choice of sauces) is $26.20.

Dearborn's excellent nut treats include Chocolate Aggies (hazelnuts dipped in dark chocolate), Cocktail Devils (roasted pecans, salted and spiced with aromatic seasonings), and Southern Dandies (roasted pecans coated with a light, golden caramel).

Conveniences: G, P, R, H **Credit Cards:** none **Shipping:** U.S.—UPS; A&H—UPS; C—UPS

DEARBORN
Dearborn Maple-Whiskey Cake

1 jar Dearborn Maple Sauce
⅔ cup raisins
½ cup whiskey
¼ pound sweet butter (room temperature)
1¼ cups packed brown sugar
3 eggs
2¼ cups flour
1 teaspoon baking soda
⅓ teaspoon salt
1 cup sour cream
⅔ cup chopped walnuts
1½ tablespoon grated orange rind

Preheat oven to 350°F. Soak raisins in ¼ cup whiskey. Grease a 9 or 10 inch Bundt pan. In mixing bowl, cream butter, then mix in Dearborn Maple Sauce and brown sugar. Beat in eggs one at a time. In another bowl, blend together flour, salt, and baking soda.

To butter mixture, add flour mixture in three additions, alternating with sour cream. Beat well after each addition. Fold in the chopped nuts, remaining whiskey, grated orange rind, and raisins with their liquid.

Pour into greased Bundt pan. Bake 1 hour or until toothpick inserted in center comes out clean. Remove from oven and cool in pan 10 minutes. Invert pan onto cake rack. Cool cake to room temperature before removing from pan. Serve plain or dust with powdered sugar.

Dearborn

Grand Finale

200 Hillcrest Road, Berkeley, California 94705

415·655·8414

*A*s of this writing, Grand Finale is California's smallest licensed candy factory, operating as it does out of Barbara Holzrichter's basement kitchen in Berkeley. But this will certainly change before long, because Ms. Holzrichter's buttercream caramels and cream dessert sauces are, in a word, outstanding.
When you read the lists of ingredients on Holzrichter's sauces and candies, it seems impossibly simple. For example, her Premium Buttercream Caramel Sauce contains sugar, cream, butter, and Madagascar Vanilla. That's it. To her Bourbon Pecan Caramel Sauce, she adds only Kentucky bourbon and pecans. It sounds simple, alright, but it isn't. Barbara knows that even a slight change in humidity can drastically alter the caramel texture and ruin a batch. That's why she keeps her batches small and watches over each with eagle eyes. To our ultimate delectation!
Grand Finale Caramels come in five flavors: Cream, Almond, Mocha, Chocolate, and Bourbon Pecan. They come in eight-ounce boxes, with a two-box minimum order for $11.65, shipping included. The Butter Caramel and Chocolate Dessert Sauces are available in seven flavors, including Cream Caramel, Caramel Macadamia Nut, Milk Chocolate Macadamia, Bourbon Pecan Caramel, Chocolate Grand Marnier, Triple Chocolate Fudge, and Creme de Menthe Chocolate. A minimum order of any two ten-ounce jars sells for $11.65, shipping included. Grand Finale also offers a beautiful handcrafted wooden gift box, which can contain either two jars of sauce or one pound of caramels. It sells for $15.95, shipping included.

Conveniences: G, P, H, D **Credit Cards:** AE, CB, DC, MC, V **Shipping:** U.S.—UPS; A&H—R; C—R

Grand Finale

Pan Handler Products

4580 Maple Street, Waterbury Center, Vermont 05677
802·244·5597

*P*atty Girouard is yet another of that special new breed, the Vermont fancy-food entrepreneur. She started by concocting in her home kitchen a tantalizing variety of interesting new fruit-and-nut conserves, many of them liquor-based. She sold seventeen thousand jars in her first year of business—and that was just the beginning.

Girouard's line of Vermont Harvest Conserves includes Strawberry Amaretto, Blueberry Bourbon, Cranapple Maple, Apple Blueberry, Brandied Peach, Apple Rum Walnut, Raspberry Apple, and Peach Melba. All are made by hand in small batches the old-fashioned way, with no additives or preservatives. They come in eight-ounce jars and sell for $3.75 each, plus shipping. Or, if you're thinking of a gift, Patty's Three Conserve Basket fits the bill nicely. Your choice of three conserves go in a handsome, reusable wicker basket for $16.00, plus shipping. Pan Handler products are also available at Marshall Field's, Macy's, and Bloomingdale's.

Conveniences: G, P, H, D **Credit Cards:** MC, V ($10.00) **Shipping:** U.S.—UPS; A&H—UPS

Polly Jean's Pantry

Polly Jean's Pantry

4561 Mission Gorge Place, Suite #K, San Diego, California 92120
619·283·5429 or 1·800·621·0852, ext. 289

*B*efore you even taste the goodness from Polly Jean's Pantry, you'll fall in love with the simple, elegant packaging. The filled mason jars sport a single gold cord with a tie-on tag of serving ideas. The white label looks as if the sauces have received a gold medal of honor, a design that matches the quality of the product.
Jean Applin and Johanna Seignious started the company in 1981 with a very good, basic chunky Chutney. The Blueberries Cassis and Cherries Jubilee (in cognac) sauces followed, with the hearty St. Ives Relish; and the beautiful White Chocolate and Dark Chocolate sauces and the Sauce à L'orange were added in 1984.
Polly Jean's doesn't normally offer mail order to individuals, but the Brookstone catalog (see Appendix 1) has wisely chosen to carry their pantry line. Or you can spring for a case (twelve to a pack) of the eight-ounce or sixteen-ounce jars ($72 and $168 respectively, not including shipping). Order early for Christmas; the East Coast deadline is November 15, and other locations should not be far behind. If you'd rather start out with a single jar, try Neiman-Marcus, I. Magnin, J.W. Robinson, and Nordstroms department stores.
Conveniences: D, G, H, P, R **Credit Cards:** none **Shipping:** U.S.—UPS; A&H—UPS; C—UPS

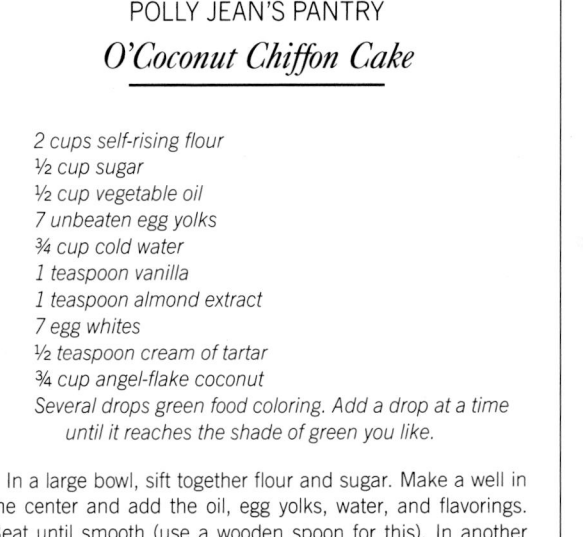

POLLY JEAN'S PANTRY
O'Coconut Chiffon Cake

2 cups self-rising flour
½ cup sugar
½ cup vegetable oil
7 unbeaten egg yolks
¾ cup cold water
1 teaspoon vanilla
1 teaspoon almond extract
7 egg whites
½ teaspoon cream of tartar
¾ cup angel-flake coconut
Several drops green food coloring. Add a drop at a time
until it reaches the shade of green you like.

In a large bowl, sift together flour and sugar. Make a well in the center and add the oil, egg yolks, water, and flavorings. Beat until smooth (use a wooden spoon for this). In another bowl, beat egg whites with the cream of tartar. Beat on high speed until very stiff peaks form. Do not underbeat. Fold in egg yolk mixture. Do not stir. Carefully fold in the coconut. Bake in a tube pan 55 minutes in a 325°F preheated oven. Increase temperature to 350°F and bake 10–15 minutes longer. Turn upside down until cold. Unmold and ice with Polly Jean's Pantry White Chocolate Velvet (at room temperature).

St. Möritz Chocolatier

506 Madison Avenue, New York, New York 10022

212·486·0266

*S*t. Möritz's most clever product comes in a shampoo tube. It looks as if it should be on the bathroom shelf, but the filling insists that it stay in the kitchen. Rich, dark, gooey chocolate, the fudge sauce can be heated in a pan of hot water and then squeezed on ice cream, cakes, and more. (Don't squeeze it onto your fingers, folks—purposefully or accidentally—it's hot.) A ten-ounce tube sells for $10.00.

Sportsmen, kids, computer buffs—they'll all find something they like from St. Möritz. A set of four solid chocolate golf balls in a wooden gift box goes for $12.00. The chocolate computer, a three-quarter-pound solid chocolate confection, can be decorated with any brief message; you can request "Happy Byte Day" or "Take a Byte." Packaged in a wooden tray, its price is set at $15.00. Or, you might want a life-size necktie in chocolate that can be monogrammed ($25.00), matched with a one-pound solid chocolate greeting card, or decorated with a personal eight-to-ten-word message ($22.00). How about a twelve-inch-high, three-pound solid chocolate teddy bear ($30.00)?

Purists, however, will opt for the truffles, a one-pound selection of heaven packed in a wooden crate for $25.00.

Write for information on the full St. Möritz line, which also includes a good cocoa powder. Although the company does not have a holiday deadline, they caution customers to order early.

Conveniences: R (with cocoa powder) **Credit Cards:** AE, MC, V **Shipping:** U.S.—UPS; A&H—UPS; C—UPS

Top Hat Company   St. Möritz Chocolatier

Top Hat Company

1245 Astor Street, Chicago, Illinois 60610

312·280·0130

*A*s chocoholics will debate over the perfect brownie, they will hotly argue about the best hot fudge sauce. Some slide smoothly over the cold ice cream; others harden; Top Hat™ becomes chewy. Reminiscent of old-fashioned neighborhood ice-cream parlors, Top Hat's jars are topped with brown-and-white striped cloth and a silver elastic bow; a tall, silk top-hat design floats above the name.

Made with corn syrup, sugar, heavy cream, cocoa, butter, chocolate, and pure vanilla extract, this sweet sauce inspired a child to remark, "That spoon is in heaven," when he saw the utensil sitting in a jar of Top Hat. For variations on a theme, try the Mint Fudge, Mocha Fudge, and Raspberry Fudge in addition to a delectable Butterscotch. All are available in twenty-ounce jars for $9.50 postage paid, except the raspberry, which sells for $10.00. The classics—hot fudge, butterscotch, and raspberry fudge—also come in ten-ounce jars for $5.50, $5.50, and $6.00, respectively. Chicago denizens will find the toppings at Marshall Fields and Neiman-Marcus; New Yorkers, at Macy's.

Conveniences: D **Credit Cards:** none **Shipping:** U.S.—R, UPS; A&H—UPS; C—UPS

BRIAN LEATART

CHAPTER FOUR

*Cookies, Cakes and
Other Desserts*

Byrd Cookie Company

2233 Naorwood Avenue P.O. Box 13086 Savannah, Georgia 31406

912·355·1716

*I*n addition to making fine cookies, biscuits, and cocktail treats, Byrd Cookie Company has long been in the business of preserving southern traditions. All of their fancy quality products, both sweet and savory, are based on authentic recipes of the Old South and are executed with the care that made southern cooking famous.

Perhaps the most unusual and indigenous of the company's products are those made with benne seeds, a spicy relative of the sesame seed that first arrived in this country by way of the African slave trade. A handful of benne seeds was a slave's most valued possession, as it was believed to be the secret of health and good luck. Byrd Cookie Company makes a tangy sweet cookie with benne seed called Benne Wafers. They come in a square eight-ounce tin for $6.50. Benne Bits are a spicy cheese cocktail bit with a subtle, appetizing flavor that's unique. They, too, come in a square eight-ounce tin for $6.50. Or, order both the Benne Bits and Wafers in a Twin Pack—sixteen ounces for $12.00.

Byrd Cookie Company's Carriage Fancy Assortment is an excellent mix of fancy gourmet cookies and cocktail tidbits. It comes in an attractive one-and-a-half-pound, ten-inch-diameter round tin for $12.00.

Conveniences: G, H **Credit Cards:** none **Shipping:** U.S.—UPS; A&H—R; C—R

Byrd Cookie Company

Cafe Beaujolais Bakery

Cafe Beaujolais Bakery

P.O. Box 730 Mendocino, California 95460

707·964·0292

*P*anforte is probably one of Western civilization's oldest surviving fancy foods. Originally made during the Middle Ages, this confection was carried by the Crusaders to provide high-energy nourishment on their travels throughout the Middle East. Since then, panforte has become a delicacy one eats at tea time, or with espresso, dessert wines, or brandy. It is a heavy, dense yet delicate cake, thickly studded with roasted nuts. It is sweet and spicy, and delightfully flavored with finely grated orange and lemon peel, both candied and fresh. Slice it in thin wedges and serve with afternoon tea for an exquisite old-world accent.

As old as it is, panforte is pretty much a rarity in this country. Margaret Fox keeps the tradition alive for us, up in Mendocino, California, at her Cafe Beaujolais Bakery. She calls hers Panforte di Mendocino, and surely it rivals the best panfortes of the world.

Cafe Beaujolais Bakery offers four varieties of Panforte di Mendocino, including almond, walnut, hazelnut, and macadamia. They each come in twenty-two-ounce wheels, with almond and walnut selling for about $18.00, the hazelnut for about $19.00, and the macadamia for approximately $24.00. They are also available at Macy's (California) and I. Magnin.

Conveniences: G, P, H, D **Credit Cards:** AE, MC, V **Shipping:** U.S.—UPS; A&H—UPS; C—UPS

The Famous Pacific Dessert Company

420 East Denny Way   Seattle, Washington 98122

206·328·1950

"*E*at dessert first . . . Life is uncertain" is the motto of this Seattle company, and it would seem their devotion to the final course is pure. Consider that their primary product—an incredibly rich, thick, chocolate cake, or gateau, or what you will—is called simply Chocolate Decadence. Evidently, further specification is extraneous. Yes, it's real, you actually eat it, but apparently it manages to transcend to the ethereal, to a richness intangible, to decadence itself.

Chocolate Decadence is made from the finest semisweet chocolate, sweet butter, fresh whole eggs, and pinches of sugar and flour. An absolute delight by itself, Chocolate Decadence can, believe it or not, be enhanced by the Pacific Dessert Company's Raspberry Purée. The combination, topped with whipped cream, is simple, elegant, and unbeatably delicious. Chocolate Decadence is available in a six-inch gift pack for $12.50 or a nine-inch restaurant size for $17.95. Raspberry Purée is sold at $6.50 for a fifteen-ounce Gift Jar. There is a $1.50 handling charge on all orders, and shipping charges depend on destination.

Conveniences: H, G, P, D **Credit Cards:** MC, V **Shipping:** U.S.—UPS; A&H—R: C—R

The Famous Pacific Dessert Company

Jake's Famous Products

401 Southwest 12th Street, Portland, Oregon 97205
503·226·1420

*I*t cuts like cheesecake, tastes of rich cocoa, and melts in the mouth. Jake's Chocolate Truffle Cake satisfies the cravings of serious chocoholics; its major ingredients are pure chocolate, butter—not margarine—and whole eggs. Attractively packaged in an octagonal box, the ready-to-serve dessert makes a nice gift item. The larger, sixteen-ounce size disappears quickly at dinner parties and buffets (proved many times over by these authors), and the four-ounce, baby version makes a great stocking stuffer for early-rising Santas (the cake should be kept refrigerated until time to cut into it). Like Jake's other products (see page 87), the truffle cake is available not from the company itself but rather from numerous mail-order catalogs. Use the address above for obtaining current information on where the cakes are offered.

Marge's Country Kitchen, Inc.

Route 1, Box 164A, Duncan, Oklahoma 73533
405·255·0753

*D*on't be surprised when you see Marge Murray's Pound Cake arrive wrapped in plain aluminum foil and plastic wrap. It's keeping her bundt-shaped cake "delicious and moist with the rich old-time goodness of country cookin' "—just as her card says. Marge Murray's break came when, thinking about a mail-order business, she wrote to Amy Vanderbilt, asking her to evaluate the blue-ribbon cake. The doyenne of etiquette responded: "I served your cake to eight guests, and it was a sensational success."
The recipe—a secret—originally came from Mrs. Murray's mother's files. Marge and her mother then adapted it to the present formula. Gene Benton described the golden dessert in *Bon Appetit* magazine as "an unusual cross between a pound cake and a Genoese cake." It keeps well and is as good toasted as it is at room temperature. Try a slice with fresh fruit or jam.
The four-pound cake will cost you $11.95 if it's shipped in the contiguous United States. Orders to Alaska, Hawaii, and Canada are more. If you want the cake for Christmas, please make sure your request is at Marge's Country Kitchen by December 7. She's already receiving almost as many orders as she can humanly handle, so the earlier the better.

Conveniences: H, P **Credit Cards:** none **Shipping:** U.S.—R, UPS; A&H—R, X, UPS; C—R, X, UPS

Moravian Sugar Crisp Company, Inc.

Route 2, Clemmons, North Carolina 27012
919·764·1402

*T*hink Valentine's Day, and you'll think flowers and candy. This year add Evva and Travis Hanes' heart-shaped Moravian ginger crisps to win someone's affection. At the very least, you'll show evidence of good taste, for these cookies are as elegant and delightfully toothsome as a cookie can be. Paper thin and nearing perfection, the crisps are mixed, rolled, and cut by hand. The secret is the elbow grease. The Haneses make a point of not selling to many stores; they want to keep quality control at its peak. Wholesale orders would increase the business but diminish the personal attention of all involved. Travis even loads the trucks sometimes.
The crisps are gaining a widespread reputation—ginger, sugar, chocolate, butterscotch, and lemon are the reasons why. Just the fragrance of the ginger cookies will set your mouth tingling; the blend of cinnamon, nutmeg, ginger, and cloves represents true Moravian tradition. And the sugar cookies' recipe dates back at least two generations in Evva's family. Each one-pound tin of assorted shapes (the hearts are included here) sells for $11.00; the two-pound tin is $18.00. The tins make great presents, but you can also order gift packs: two one-pound tins of ginger and sugar cookies are $20.00. Add a one-pound tin of chocolate crisps and the price goes up to $29.00. With another one-pound tin of lemon crisps, it's $38.00. All five flavors (one pound each) are available for $45.00. Shipping is included, excluding Alaska and Hawaii, which require an additional $4.00. Holiday orders must be received by December 10, and if you're paying by check, make it payable to Mrs. Travis F. Hanes.

Conveniences: G, H, P **Credit Cards:** none **Shipping:** U.S.—UPS; A&H—R

Neal's Cookies

423 Southwest Freeway, Houston, Texas 77002

713·520·6602 or 1·800·847·0096

Neal Elinoff left medical school to become a professional cookie maker, so you know he's a serious man. If you doubt it, just try his cookies. Anything that tastes as good as Neal's Cookies can't be taken lightly. As further proof, Elinoff makes his own chocolate, so conscientious is he about the quality of his cookies. He actually grinds his own cocoa beans, refines them, and delicately "conches" them for 72 hours like the Swiss do, until his chocolate is creamier and richer than any other. Neal's Chocolate is so good, it's become a whole other business in itself, but that's another story.

Neal offers a great variety of his homemade-style cookies, including Milk Chocolate with Pecans, Chocolate Chunk, Oatmeal Raisin, White Chocolate with Macadamia Nut, Peanut Butter Chocolate Chunk, and Chocolate Walnut Chocolate Chunk. They come in a one-and-a-half-pound gift box for $10.50, plus $5.50 shipping, or in a handsome one-and-a-half-pound round tin for $14.50, plus shipping.

Conveniences: G, D **Credit Cards:** AE **Shipping:** U.S.—X; A&H—X; C—X

Neal's Cookies

Moravian Sugar Crisp Company, Inc.

39

Owl Enterprises, Inc.

NEW ENGLAND DAIRY FOODS
398-400 Pine Street, Burlington, Vermont 05401
802·864·7271 or 1·800·447·1205

*T*hey call this cheesecake crazy and mixed-up, but there is no confusion about its excellent quality, extreme rich taste, or smooth velvety texture. Without doubt, this is one of the finest cheesecakes in the country.
They call it crazy, of course, because each cheesecake is a mixture of four different varieties: Strawberry Swirl, Black Forest Cherry, Plain, and Fudge Swirl. The key ingredient, say Vermont Velvet makers, is their fresh cream cheese, which is delivered daily from nearby dairy farms. And the experts concur: *Gourmet* magazine called Vermont Velvet Cheesecake "a velvet-soft monument to American cream cheese."
Each cheesecake weighs a whopping four pounds, ten ounces and comes precut into sixteen slices. They last an easy three weeks in the refrigerator, or they can be frozen on delivery without any loss of quality or texture.
One mixed-up cheesecake is $25.00 from November to March, $29.99 from April to November 1 (slightly more for Hawaii). Or you can order a plain cheesecake for $20.00 from November to March, $25.00 April to November. Whole cheesecakes are also available in any of the above flavors, or Chocolate, Kahlua, or Amaretto.
Conveniences: P, H **Credit Cards:** none **Shipping:** U.S.—UPS 2nd Day Air

The Postilion

The Postilion

615 Old Pioneer Road, Fond du Lac, Wisconsin 54935
414·922·4170

*M*adame Kuony's Plum Pudding and Hard Sauce have earned a well-deserved international reputation for excellence. Made with only the very best ingredients, the two crown a Christmas table the way few desserts can. Madame Kuony makes mouths water when she describes her renowned delicacy: "We steep choice fruits and almonds in French cognac, then combine them with spices and fresh eggs whipped to a foam with Irish stout. That's what our plum puddings are made of." She neglected to add that the bread for the crumbs is made in her kitchen—further proof of the personal attention every item receives from this gracious French restaurateur.
The hard sauce is exquisite. Newly churned, unsalted butter; a neighboring farm's eggs; cognac; and rum combine to form a gourmet's delight. A one-pound pudding with hard sauce ($17.50) serves eight. The two-and-a-half-pound pudding and larger jar of hard sauce ($30.00) serves twelve to fifteen.
This, and other Postilion treats, come with gift boxes if you request it. They will include a card of your choice, as long as it measures three-by-five inches or smaller. If you'd rather, they'll enclose a gift card with your message. For a special family or friend, send Our Original Christmas Box, a handsome package with tasty trimmings that will never reach the tree: plum pudding and hard sauce to serve six, and large one-and-a-quarter-pound jars of Apricot-Prune and Cherry-Pineapple compotes ($35.00). Christmas orders should be in by December 1 at the latest.
For shipments west of Denver add five percent to the prices above. Department store shoppers can find Madame Kuony's products at Neiman-Marcus, Marshall Fields, and I. Magnin.
Conveniences: D, G, H **Credit Cards:** none **Shipping:** U.S.—UPS; A&H—UPS; C—UPS

Rowena's and Captain Jaap's

758 West 22nd Street, Norfolk, Virginia 23517

804·627·8699

*W*e won't go on and on about Rowena's Almond Pound Cake. Suffice to say that this two-and-three-quarters-pound beauty has thrown many a diet. The label advises to slice the cake very thinly ("it is deliciously rich"), but a weighty slab of it is just as good. Toast it with butter for breakfast or just indulge—top it with vanilla ice cream and caramel sauce. The cake's dense moistness brings great satisfaction.

Although the cake is marketed under Rowena's label, the recipe originated with Captain Joseph Jaap's mother. Quality and care are clearly the founding principles of Rowena's and Captain Jaap's products (see also page 26). A perfect housewarming gift, the cake comes wrapped in cellophane with a red-and-white polka dot bow. You may send a card to be enclosed, or the company will include in each gift a handwritten card with your own message on it.

The gem sells for $11.50.

Conveniences: D, P **Credit Cards:** Choice, MC, V **Shipping:** U.S.—UPS; A&H—UPS; C—UPS

The Postilion

*M*adame Kuony is an imposing, gracious woman with a great deal of presence. Her foods reflect her personality. Without boasting, she can say that she has the best mail-order plum pudding and hard sauce in the United States. With a dedication to using only prime-quality ingredients, Madame Kuony began producing her specialty foods just over thirty years ago, a little more than a year after she and her husband opened a small French restaurant in Fond du Lac, Wisconsin. The Postilion is ever thriving in its early Victorian homestead. The twenty-eight-guest restaurant reserves tables months in advance, catering to an international clientele, many of whom are respected for their knowledge of good food and wine. Madame Kuony's mail-order delicacies—standouts in the world of special comestibles—are prepared with the same exacting care as are the foods in her kitchen.

Rowena's and Captain Jaap's

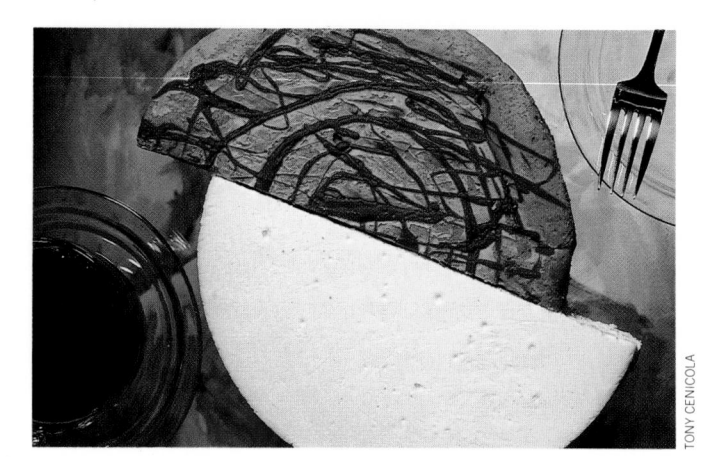

The Sweetery

The Sweetery

1816 East Greenville Street, Anderson, South Carolina 29621

803·224·8394

*W*hen you think about it, that you can get the extraordinary homemade treats of this tiny South Carolina bakery delivered to your home, ready to eat, in a matter of two days, it revives a certain faith in the modern world. Truly, the Sweetery produces what must be some of the best desserts in this country, and certainly some of the finest available by mail order. Take, for example, their specialty, the Uggly Cake. It is a rich layer of fine yellow cake sandwiched with a creamy caramel-flavored nut custard—on the whole not much to look at, perhaps, but altogether ethereal against the palate. The eight-inch cake weighs one and a half pounds and sells for $8.00 with a two-cake minimum order.

Jane Jarahian opened the Sweetery after a fruitless search for a quality bakery that offered home-baked goodies "a la Americana." Making good use of local southern cooking talents, Jarahian now employs housewives in her kitchen. Their baking know-how, and the best fresh ingredients available, are the simple combination that makes the Sweetery's goodies unbeatable.

Among the Sweetery's other offerings are Brownies 'n' Cream, a moist cake brownie of dark chocolate swirled with thick white cream cake; a great Amaretto Chocolate Chip Cookie; and a rich Pecan Cookie Bar that, bite for bite, rivals the best cookies of the world. The Sweetery's Carolina Cheesecake is yet another most mentionable monument to American cookery. Each nine-inch cheesecake weighs three and three-quarter pounds and sells for $18.50. It also comes in a delicious Chocolate Amaretto variation for $19.95.

Conveniences: G, P, H **Credit Cards:** MC, V **Shipping:** U.S.—UPS; A&H—UPS; C—UPS

Wick's Pies

217 Greenville Avenue, Winchester, Indiana 47394

317·584·8401

*D*uane Wickersham was named Indiana's Small Businessman of the Year in 1967. His list of accomplishments centered around one product: Sugar Cream Pie, based on his grandmother's recipe. Throughout his career, Wick tried to improve his business, and succeeded; he didn't try to improve the pie. He knew he had something special—so special, in fact, that he tried to patent the pie, twice traveling to Washington, D.C., to do so.

The pie's ingredients are simple—just what you'd think would go into a sugar cream pie—but the result is what now seems to be called a comfort food, a good, old-fashioned throwback to times past that still stands up to today's sophisticated poached pear kiwi cobblers and chocolate truffle mousse cakes.

Practicalities are in order when mailing away for these pies. The Thanksgiving deadline is November 1; Christmas, December 1. Shipping is extra—$8.50 for UPS Second Day Air and $28.50 for UPS Next Day Air—an unfortunate addition to these relatively inexpensive pies ($12.00 for a case of six).

Conveniences: H **Credit Cards:** MC, V **Shipping:** U.S.—UPS Air

CHAPTER FIVE

Candies

<u>*ACME Candy Company*</u>

4839 Don Drive, Dallas, Texas 75247

214·634·2825

*A*CME Candy Company is a large manufacturer of premium-quality, Creole-style candies. While they sell their products primarily on a wholesale basis, they do sell by mail order during the Christmas season, and the rest of the year their products are available through Goodies from Goodman catalog.

Quite a number of ACME's specialty candies are unique and well worth seeking out. For example, they have quality pralines in four delicious flavors including Rum, Chocolate, Maple, and Pecan. Another of their specialties is frosted pecans, which come in Rum, Chocolate, Cinnamon, Orange, Praline, Bourbon, and Piña Colada flavors. They are all excellent, and they are inexpensive when compared to other fancy regional candies.

The Frosted Pecans come in one-pound or seven-ounce jars, or in one- , two- , or three-pound tins and are available in gift-jar assortments. ACME candies can also be found at Sanger-Harris department stores.

Conveniences: G, D **Credit Cards:** none **Shipping:** U.S.—UPS; C—R

<u>*Beach Candy Company Inc.*</u>

P.O. Box 1997, Pinehurst, North Carolina 28374

919·692·3401

*H*ere's a company that has kept things refreshingly simple. Malinda Kitchin developed a delicious new candy in her home in Virginia Beach, Virginia. It's a dark-chocolate-covered Almond Buttercrunch that's harder than an ordinary buttercrunch but softer than toffee. In 1981, Malinda started to sell her candy—she called them Sinful candies—and people loved and bought them. Malinda made more, and people bought more. She didn't change a thing or add to her line. She just kept making her Almond Crunches. Now, Sinful candies are sold all over the United States and Canada, as well as in England, Spain, Germany, and Portugal. Success was simple.

Kitchin has branched out since moving her kitchens to Pinehurst, North Carolina, early in 1985, though only modestly. Her same special Almond Crunch is now offered with a white chocolate coating, too. Both Sinful versions are superb and addictive. White and dark chocolate Sinful candies come in four sizes: 12.9 ounces (forty-five pieces) at $18.95; 8.9 ounces (thirty pieces) at $12.50; 4.9 ounces (fifteen pieces) at $7.95; and a small sampler at $5.25. There is no minimum order, and all sizes are beautifully packaged in black shiny boxes with white or red ribbon.

Conveniences: G, P, H **Credit Cards:** MC, V **Shipping:** U.S.—UPS; A&H—R; C—R (Ontario only)

The Brigittine Monks

The Brigittine Monks

125 Northgate Drive, Woodside, California 94062

415·364·4267

*C*amelot exists. Not the home of King Arthur but the home of the Brigittine Monks, who just happen to make divine fudge. Brother Benedict Kirby, who acts as liaison with the outside world, writes that the fudge received a Medallion of Excellence award from *Chocolate News* magazine, which earlier declared the confection a "visual and gustatory sensation." Right they are. This fudge exceeds any we've ever tasted—and that includes homemade.

Free of preservatives and additives, the chocolate fudge consists of blended Guittard chocolate, sweet butter, pure vanilla, and a seemingly magical ingredient called Mazetta, a marshmallow creme that accounts for the fudge's unusually smooth texture. The Pecan-Praline Fudge Royale label reads "Pecans" at the beginning of its list of ingredients. Plain and Pecan-Praline are the two flavors for purists.

The one-pound boxes ($10.00 each) also include Chocolate with Nuts, Chocolate Mint, Chocolate Amaretto, and Divinity Fudge. Also part of the brothers' repertoire is a selection of truffles—chocolate, assorted chocolate, and assorted iced—which sells for $8.00 (for a seven-and-a-half-ounce package). The truffles, sadly, are available only October through April.

These treats can be found at Macy's in California, Neiman-Marcus, and I. Magnin. And, if you're ordering from Alaska, Hawaii, or Puerto Rico, please include an additional $5.00. Although there are no gift packages, you can ask that a card be included with the order if it's being sent to someone other than the purchaser. The last note may not come as a surprise; the brothers *do* have a holiday deadline: December 18.

Conveniences: D, H **Credit Cards:** none **Shipping:** U.S.—UPS; A&H—UPS; C—R

Buckley's English Toffee, Inc.

Buckley's English Toffee, Inc.

Box 14119, Baton Rouge, Louisiana 70898-4119

504·642·8381

*I*n a handsome 1920s-style cream, brown, and black tin, Buckley's English Toffee hails from Sunshine, Louisiana. M.S. Buckley cooked up his first batch of this crunchy mouthwatering sweet in Newton, Mississippi, in 1958 to raise money for his church. A can made its way to Atlanta, and Buckley's had its first mail-order customer. The toffee-making tradition has now passed on to the next generation.

Made from butter, sugar, margarine, and almonds, the buttery-tasting candy has no added preservatives. A two-pound tin of the delightfully thin one-inch squares will run you $8.95, plus shipping, which depends on destination.

Conveniences: P **Credit Cards:** MC, V **Shipping:** U.S.—R, UPS; A&H—R, UPS; C—R, UPS

Champlain Chocolate Company

416 Pine Street, Burlington, Vermont 05401

802·864·1808

*F*ew American companies have yet to master the ultimate chocolate-making challenge that is the truffle—that smooth, creamy, delicate queen of confections. The Champlain Chocolate Company has done it, and with aplomb. The delightful creations of this small Vermont company are convincing testimony to the fact that the new American gourmet chocolates are quickly approaching the levels of the great chocolates of Belgium, France, and Holland.

It was just this lack of competent American truffle-making that prompted chef Tad Spurgeon to go into the truffle business with his friend James Lampman, a Burlington restaurant owner. First, the team got the best ingredients they could find—100 percent Callebaut chocolate from Belgium, pure Vermont heavy cream, and sweet butter. Their next step—and it's a long one—is to make all their truffles completely by hand, assuring special attention to the taste and visual aesthetic of each piece. The result is a rich, though quite light, truffle that's scrumptious.

Champlain Chocolate Company offers their assorted American Truffles in a seven-ounce size, at $12.00; or thirteen ounces, at $22.50. They also feature a variety of excellent Chocolates of Vermont, which includes Honey Caramel, Almond/Raisin, Evergreen Mint, and Maple Crunch flavors. These come in a 7.8-ounce box for $11.00 or a 14.7-ounce box for $19.50.

Conveniences: G, P, H, D **Credit Cards:** AE, MC, V **Shipping:** U.S.—UPS; A&H—X; C—R, X

Champlain Chocolate Company

Creole Delicacies Company

533 St. Ann Street, New Orleans, Louisiana 70116

504·525·9508

The word praline has been attached to a diverse variety of confections and desserts, but who knows what an authentic pecan praline really is like? Creole Delicacies of New Orleans does. They've been making an extraordinarily rich, creamy pecan praline for over thirty years, from a recipe that can be traced to the court of Louis XIV.

Located in the heart of the New Orleans French Quarter, facing historic Jackson Square, Creole Delicacies Company makes their pralines fresh each day, simmering the precious mixture in large copper kettles, pouring them by hand and packing each individually in heat-sealed packets for freshness.

Pecan Pralines are available in the Original (brown sugary) flavor, or Rum or Chocolate flavors. A handsome twelve-ounce box is $9.95, postage included; the Original flavor comes in a six-ounce box at $7.50.

Creole Delicacies also offers a delectable item they call Pecanfections, which are huge praline-encrusted pecans—$10.95 per eight-ounce jar; as well as a rich Praline Topping, priced at $15.95 for three ten-ounce jars.

Conveniences: G, P, H **Credit Cards:** AE, MC, V **Shipping:** U.S.—R, UPS

Creole Delicacies Company

Cummings Studio Chocolates

679 East 600 South, Salt Lake City, Utah 84105

801·328·4858

This small company has maintained a commitment to making the best chocolate it is possible to make, since 1924, when V. Clyde Cummings turned his hobby into a business. Clyde had started making chocolates at the age of fifteen, and after painstaking and protracted experimentation, eventually devised what today remains the company's "Secret Process." Sole heir to the treasurable recipes and methods was Clyde's son Paul, who for the last twenty years has made all the candy under carefully sequestered conditions, leaving only the cutting and dipping to others.

Cummings Studio Chocolates include a delightful variety of superb centers—creamy smooth and soft, chewy, with nuts and without—that are guaranteed to satisfy discriminating chocoholics. And the chocolate they use is the famous South American Tehuantepec kind, so expensive that only one or two other chocolate makers in the country use it.

Cummings offers two chocolate packages—a dreamy delight they call the Neapolitan Opera Bar and their famous Assorted Chocolates. Both are available in one-pound, two-pound, three-pound, and five-pound boxes, which come gift-wrapped. They cost $11.25, $20.00, $29.00, and $46.75, respectively. The company does not ship during hot summer months.

Conveniences: G, P **Credit Cards:** AE, MC, V **Shipping:** U.S.—R, UPS; A&H—R, UPS; C—R, UPS

Cummings Studio Chocolates

Ethel M Chocolates

Ethel M Chocolates

P.O. Box 18413, Las Vegas, Nevada 89015

702·458·8864 or 1·800·634·6584

*I*t may well be worth the trip to Nevada to try Ethel M Liqueurs; it's one of the few states that permits manufacture of liqueur-filled chocolates. If you're housebound, you'll still be able to delight in Ethel M's other confections. Her Deluxe Assortment is a two-pound package of her best mouthwatering goodies ($25.00). The one-pound Dark Chocolate and Milk Chocolate Assortments sell for $11.00 each, as do the boxes of Raspberry Butter Creams, Lemon Creams, and Pecan Patties.

"One must practice at keeping the manifestation of his happiness restrained to an inner glow," recommends Ethel M's rules of etiquette for enjoying fine chocolates in company. "Do not roll your eyes no matter how wonderfully delicious the chocolate is." Made with fresh butter, corn syrup, and double grade A eggs, Ethel M's creations—all-American in flavor— are packed in a buff-colored box with a simple gold-cord tie: an elegant package sure to please Mother on her day, the folks at the office, or that someone special.

Holiday orders should be at the address above by December 15, or, if you're in Arizona, California, or Nevada, you can stop in at one of the company's thirty-two shoppes. All-occasion and Christmas wrappings are available on request.

Conveniences: G, H, P, R **Credit Cards:** AE, MC, V **Shipping:** U.S.—X; A&H—X; C—X

Harbor Sweets

Box 150, Marblehead, Massachusetts 01945

617·745·7648

*H*arbor Sweets, a small company actually operating out of Salem, Massachusetts, has come up with one of the most unique, truly sweet ideas of the decade: a large Christmas calendar box with small doors that open onto an assortment of delectable chocolates. The Advent-type calendar shows a pastel-colored town complete with snowy New England streets that reach down to the shore, an appropriate seaside theme for this cottage industry that produces candies named Sweet Sloops®, Sand Dollars®, Sweet Shells™, and Barque Sarah™. And although Marblehead Mints® lacks an overtly nautical title, these are tiny sailboats "embossed on a sea of bittersweet chocolate delicately flavored with peppermint starlights." An apt description: These mints will encourage even the most curmudgeonly sweet tooth to wax poetic.

The Sweet Sloops are our favorite, though. Toffee lovers will appreciate this theme candy. The sloop is almond butter crunch, her mainsail and jib are coated in white chocolate, and the sea on which she sails is dark chocolate sprinkled with pecan spindrift—the most delicious sea spray you'll ever come across.

The company's catalog offers treasures and pleasures too numerous to name—all variations of chocolates and gift items, including among others Dedham Pottery-style containers, rosebud wreaths, and a Maine wind-bell. The chocolates do run on the expensive side—$14.00 to $25.00 for a red gift box postpaid—but they are well worth it. The Sweet Sloops, Marblehead Mints, and Sweet Shells come thirty pieces to the box; the larger candies, Barque Sarah Miniatures and Sand Dollars, have sixteen and fifteen to the box, respectively. Double the numbers for the big boxes, which are $26.00 to $28.00 postpaid. Air, Express, and foreign orders will be billed.

Conveniences: D, G, P **Credit Cards:** AE, MC, V **Shipping:** U.S.—UPS; A&H—R, UPS; C—R

Harbor Sweets

*H*arbor Sweets find their way into the crème de la crème of magazines; articles featuring the candies have popped up in *Town & Country, Travel & Leisure,* and *Gourmet.* And with good reason. Ben Strohecker, a former marketing director of Schrafft's, makes great chocolates *and* he knows how to find the best homes for his sweets.

After *Gourmet* recognized Strohecker as one of the leading chocolatiers in North America, the Boston Museum of Fine Arts approached Harbor Sweets; the museum wanted to feature the confections in its Christmas catalog and in its shop. Strohecker moved on instinct and proposed that he make a chocolate to represent the museum's most popular exhibit— the Egyptian collection. It didn't take long before Strohecker and the Egyptology curator decided to make *ushabtis.* (Also called *shawabitis,* these small helpers look like mummies; their purpose was to do work in the underworld, thus saving the real mummy the toil. Hundreds might have been buried in one tomb, as many as one for each day of the year.)

Wrapped in a paper pyramid, the candies gained a wide and strong following. Not long after, other organizations requested similar services from Strohecker. His creations include miniature dinosaurs for the Carnegie Institute; miniature hard hats, again for the Boston Museum of Fine Arts; and embossed or sculpted variations of the Marblehead Mint candy for the Metropolitan Opera Company, Boston Symphony Orchestra, the Rock Resort Little Dix Bay, Sheraton Hotels, and the U.S.S. Constitution Museum, to name a few.

Harbor Sweets

Marshall's Mackinac Trail, Inc.

308 East Central Avenue, Mackinaw City, Michigan 49701

616·436·5379

*N*o preservatives. Good ingredients. An old-fashioned recipe that dates back to 1887. True fudge connoisseurs will appreciate the almost crumbly quality of this northern Michigan confection. It makes a sweet counterpoint to smooth fudges like those of the Brigittine monks (see page 45). Marshall's melts so easily on the tongue, it's a grinful, sinful treat— great for kids and picnics.

The family-owned and operated business takes great pride in making the candy daily on marble slabs under the watchful eyes of customers. More than twenty flavors are available from May through December, when the store is open. Maple English Walnut, Chocolate Cashew, Vanilla Pecan, Peanut Butter, and Chocolate Rum only begin the list.

The one-half-pound slices come two to a box for $6.00. A gift box of two slices of fudge, one pecan log (another of Marshall's famous sweets), and a half pound of sweet cream caramels runs for $9.95. Christmas orders must be received by December 6 to be filled on time.

Conveniences: G, H, P **Credit Cards:** AE, CB, DC, MC, V, ($10.00) **Shipping:** U.S.—UPS; A&H—R, UPS; C—R, UPS

Minerva Street Chocolate, Inc.

1052 Olivia, Ann Arbor, Michigan 48104

313·996·4090

*T*he experts seem to agree: When Judy Weinblatt started making chocolate truffles out of her home kitchen in 1980, the truffle in America was transformed—lifted to a whole new level of excellence. These richest of delights have been lauded by the food critics of the *Washington Post* and *Chicago Tribune,* and *Chocolatier* magazine has named Minerva Street Truffles among the ten best in the *world!*

Unlike other truffles, which are commonly oversized and too heavy, Weinblatt's little masterpieces provide the palate with a pure, super-smooth chocolate cream that is rich without being heavy. On the exterior, each truffle is an elegantly crafted, symmetrical thing of beauty.

Minerva Street Truffles come in a variety of flavors, including Vanilla Bean, Praline, Rum, Brandy, Cheesecake, Orange, Mocha, Hazelnut Crunch Caramel, and others, many of them dusted with crushed pistachios, cashews, or hazelnuts. They come in a fourteen-ounce (eighteen pieces) assortment for $24.50, plus $3.00 shipping, or you can specially order a fourteen-ounce box in all one flavor, or whatever selection you like, for $28.50, plus $3.00 shipping. Minerva Street Chocolates also features chocolate-dipped caramels. A fourteen-ounce box is $24.50, plus $3.00 shipping. All boxes are gift-wrapped in blue or red paper with a silver bow and matching gift card.

Conveniences: G, P, H **Credit Cards:** AE, MC, V **Shipping:** U.S.—UPS; A&H—R; C—UPS

Minerva Street Chocolate, Inc.

Paron Chocolatier

199 Brook Street, Scarsdale, New York 10583

914·725·5525

*P*aron Chocolatier is one of the most interesting and innovative chocolate novelty makers in America. Besides featuring an exciting and exquisite line of very fancy European-style chocolates, Harriot Sessa, the company founder and expert chocolatier, has let her imagination run amok with fresh ideas for gourmet chocolate combinations. A dark chocolate-coated caramel popcorn is one such Sessa invention, and it's sensational. Another is something of a gourmet chocolate chip cookie turned inside-out. Paron calls them Cookie Chip Chocolates; they are delicate small chunks of cookie dipped in rich dark chocolate, stuck together in bumpy cookie-sized pieces. When eaten, these special sweets bestow an enchanting reversed view of all sweetdom, roughly equivalent to viewing Earth from the moon. Cookie Chip Chocolates are mint or regular flavored, and come in a five-ounce bag for $6.00 or nine-ounce and nineteen-ounce gift boxes for $9.00 and $17.00, respectively. The Paron Popcorn comes in four-ounce, eight-ounce, and sixteen-ounce boxes for $6.00, $9.00, and $14.00.

Mail orders are filled from September 15 to June 1 only, but Paron is also available at Neiman-Marcus, Garfinkel's, Bonwit Teller, Stern's, and Food Emporium.

Conveniences: G, H, D, P **Credit Cards:** AE, MC, V **Shipping:** U.S.—UPS; A&H—UPS; C—X

Rachel's Brownies

Rachel's Brownies

105 Great Valley Parkway, Malvern, Pennsylvania 19355

**215·296·2198 or 1·800·441·7387
or 1·800·622·2444 in Pennsylvania**

*T*here are all kinds of brownies in this world, many of them quite good, but Rachel's Brownies clearly stand apart. These are serious brownies, of a richness that could almost be mistaken for a fine fudge, and even if you aren't a brownie connoisseur, you'll taste the difference in Rachel's.

Rachel Borish had no plans to become a brownie maker. In fact, she was studying to be a concert pianist when tendinitis forced her to quit. She'd been baking her brownies for friends and family for a couple of years, but never thought of selling them. Instead, they sold themselves. Rachel had reluctantly taken her sister-in-law's advice to market her brownies when, almost before she knew it, Rachel's Brownies were in such demand that she could hardly keep up with orders. Now, a mere ten years later, Rachel employs forty people, and her business grosses approximately two million dollars a year.

Rachel's Brownies now sells two kinds of brownies—the original Double Chocolate Brownies with Walnuts, and her husband's Butterscotch Brownies. Both kinds come in pretty brown boxes that contain one dozen individually wrapped two-ounce brownies. They sell for $10.00, plus $3.00 for shipping.

Conveniences: G, P **Credit Cards:** MC, V, ($10.00) **Shipping:** U.S.—UPS; A&H—R

Standard Candy Company

715 Massman Drive, Nashville, Tennessee 37210

615·889·6360

*P*icture an array of squat, color-filled glass jars on the wooden counter of a country general store at the turn of the century. They used to contain stick candy, those wonderful old-fashioned candies nobody could resist. You'd hold one in your mouth like a slender lollypop, sucking the sweetness slowly while the afternoon aged, and the day would be much better. But you can't get stick candy anymore, right? Wrong. The Standard Company still makes a premium-quality stick candy, using an original recipe that hasn't changed since 1901, when the company was founded. King Leo Stick Candy combines pure cane sugar, corn syrup, and corn sugar with four delicious flavors: Traditional Peppermint, Clove, Lemon, and Vanilla. They come in an attractive old-fashioned two-pound tin for $5.50, with each additional tin priced at $4.35.

Conveniences: P, H **Credit Cards:** MC, V, ($20.00) **Shipping:** U.S.—UPS

Standard Candy Company

That's My Favorite Inc.

That's My Favorite Inc.

1791 Blount Road #1 Bay 603, Pompano Beach, Florida 33069

305·979·3143

*W*hen Cathy Goldstein left the world of professional fashion modeling to make and market gourmet candy, she brought the bright lights and flash with her. She's got personality! And so do her candies. Each of her six candy varieties has a distinct and delicious character and all of them come boxed in jazzy, show-stopping colors with glittering braided silver string. The packaging is a knock-out, and if it doesn't get you, the candy will.

That's My Favorite is the name Goldstein gave to her original candy, a scrumptious almond butter crunch sandwiched between layers of milk chocolate and dusted with fine-ground toasted almonds. Two other of Goldstein's star candies are her Oh Heavenly, which is a marshmallow center in milk chocolate with Georgia pecans, and Rainbow Rapture, a chewy homemade taffy in honey vanilla, strawberry, chocolate, and grape flavors.

That's My Favorite comes in one-half-pound boxes—$11.50 if it's in a pink-and-blue box, $13.00 if in silver—and one-pound boxes—$18.50 in pink and blue, $19.50 in silver. Oh Heavenly comes in fourteen-ounce boxes at $14.00, and Rainbow Rapture comes in four-, six-, ten-, or twelve-ounce bags at $3.50, $4.50, $6.00, and $8.50, respectively.

Conveniences: G, P, H, D **Credit Cards:** MC, V, ($10.00) **Shipping:** U.S.—UPS; A&H—R, UPS

JOHN WILLIAM LUND

CHAPTER SIX

Nuts and Dried Fruits

The El Paso Chile Company™

100 Ruhlin Court, El Paso, Texas 79922

915·544·3434

A cigar-box-style bronzed Indian with a corncob headdress emblazons El Paso's unique Popcorn on the Cob jar. Packed in an authentic two-liter French canning jar, this popcorn may be a little pricey, but its fresh kernels—and its fresh packaging—make it a perfect gift item as a stocking stuffer, a birthday extra, or a surprise for that someone special on an otherwise ordinary day. Each jar offers a clear view of the miniature cobs. You can also get the popping corn in an attractive handmade wooden crate. Both are available for $13.00, plus delivery charges. (See page 115 for catalog and store information.)

Conveniences: D, G, P, R **Credit Cards:** MC, V **Shipping:** U.S.—R, X, UPS; A&H—R; C—R, X, UPS

Gaston Dupre, Inc.

6201 Johns Road #11, Tampa, Florida 33614

813·885·9445

*G*aston Dupre, Inc. might be a young company (it was established in 1980), but its staunch adherence to a classic recipe marks it as one that will be around for some time to come. At a time when the praline varies according to each confectioner's whim, Gaston Dupre bases its "Original Savannah Praline" on the recipe created in seventeenth-century France by none other than the chef of the Duke of Prasline, whose name the new candy borrowed. The Duke's chef made this treat by taking individual whole almonds and coating them in a crunchy roasted caramel. Gaston Dupre holds true to this French tradition that came to America while also venturing pecans, hazelnuts, and macadamias into this delightful pralinated form. They all make supreme snacking, or can be ground as a wonderful ingredient for butter creams, or as a rich topping for ice cream or a dessert filling. They come in beautiful sixteen-ounce white paper bags with a hand-tied ribbon. The Hazelnut Praline is $8.95, Almond is $9.20, Pecan is $11.00, and Macadamia is $16.50. Add $1.75 for shipping.

Conveniences: G, H, D **Credit Cards:** AE, MC **Shipping:** U.S.—UPS

The Peanut Patch

P.O. Box 186, Courtland, Virginia 23837

804·653·2028

*N*o matter how you like your peanuts—boiled, roasted, raw, blanched, in the shell, salted or unsalted—the Peanut Patch does them all ways, with a gourmet touch. If, like many people, you don't know what you prefer in a peanut, but have always trusted that peanuts were peanuts, now's your chance to experience the great possibilities of the premium peanut. The Peanut Patch starts with the best Virginia peanuts available from their native Southampton County, the world's largest peanut-producing county. Next, they usher each nut through their various time-tested cooking and salting processes to produce a truly gourmet peanut, that is one of the crunchiest, most flavorful peanuts anywhere, period.
The Peanut Patch offers a variety of gift packs. For example, their Tasty Teaser includes ten ounces of "Home-Cooked" salted peanuts and ten ounces of Home-Cooked Redskins, for $4.50. The Peanut Patch original gift pack includes one pound of Home-Cooked salted, one pound of Home-Cooked Redskins, twelve ounces of Salted-in-the-Shell, twelve ounces of Roasted-in-the-Shell, eight ounces of Chocolate Covered, seven ounces of Sugar Coated, and eight ounces of Old-Fashioned Peanut Squares. It totals seven pounds and costs $18.95. If you're throwing a big party, the Peanut Patch also sells in bulk. A twenty-five-pound box of blanched raw peanuts is $33.75, plus shipping.

Conveniences: G, P, R **Credit Cards:** AE, MC, V **Shipping:** U.S.—UPS; A&H—R; C—R, UPS

Sphinx Date Ranch Inc.

4041 E. Thomas Road, Phoenix, Arizona 85008
602·224·0195

*T*he Sphinx Medjool Date is widely known among date aficionados as the Cadillac of Dates. Outsized, moist, fiberless, meaty, dark, and tender-skinned, Medjools come from palms that are not grown from seed, but from the delicate, high-yield offshoots of the mother palm.

Rick Heetland, owner of the Sphinx Date Ranch in Phoenix, Arizona, guarantees these beautiful, plump rascals, and we cannot but stand by him. If there's such a thing as a gourmet date, and we firmly believe there is, this is it.

Sphinx Medjools are available in one-pound increments, from one to twelve pounds. A one-pound box goes for $10.95; six pounds are $34.95. Gift boxes are available, as are a variety of Sphinx Ranch specialties such as walnut-stuffed, pecan-stuffed, and chocolate-dipped dates.

Conveniences: G, R, P, H **Credit Cards:** AE, MC, V **Shipping:** U.S.—R, X, UPS

Sphinx Date Ranch Inc.

Timber Crest Farms

Timber Crest Farms

4791 Dry Creek Road, Healdsburg, California 95448

707·433·8251

*T*imber Crest Farms is approaching its thirtieth year of growing, drying, and packaging California's finest organically grown dried fruits and nuts. Ronald Waltenspiel and staff were the first to develop and market unsulfured dried fruits and nuts, which have gained wide acceptance throughout the health food and gourmet industries. All Timber Crest products are harvested when fully ripe, dried at the lowest possible temperatures, and stored in cold storage until packaging. The resultant flavor is remarkably vibrant and delicious.

In addition to consumer-size and restaurant-size packages of dried fruits and nuts, Timber Crest Farms produces a complete line of Dried Fruit and Nut gift baskets, all of which contain prunes, dates, figs, walnuts, and blanched almonds. A one-pound gift basket is $10.49, a two-pound, twelve-ounce basket is $15.22, and a five-pound Redwood Gift Box is $29.16. You can also buy these dried fruits and nuts separately. Dried apples, apricots, cherries, dates, figs (Calimyrna and Mission), papaya, peaches, pears, pineapple, prunes, raisins, star fruit, and a huge variety of nuts are all available at reasonable prices.

Conveniences: G, D, P, R **Credit Cards:** MC, V **Shipping:** U.S.—UPS; A&H—R; C—R

Timber Crest Farms

BRIAN LEATART

CHAPTER SEVEN

Spices, Herbs and Flavorings

Aspen Mulling Spices

c/o Wax & Wicks, Inc., P.O. Box 191, Aspen, Colorado 81612
303·925·3984

*K*eifer Mendenhall is a congenial man who will unabashedly tell you that his mulling spices are "the best there is." And he's right. Packaged in a milk-cartonlike six-ounce container, this blend of sugars and flavorings will transform cider, wine, tea, and brandy into an elixir that conjures up roaring fireplaces, snowy scenes, and a cozy companion.
Mendenhall, who owns Wax & Wicks, the oldest gift shop in Aspen, began brewing hot and cold spiced cider to encourage customers to linger and browse among his gift items. That was more than fifteen years ago. Now, with store sales of approximately twenty thousand cartons of mix a year, Aspen Mulling Spices has gone national and will accept mail orders. At $1.50 a carton, plus shipping, the fragrant package makes a nice stocking stuffer.
Even purists will agree that a mulled mix that dissolves immediately and doesn't need to simmer is a boon to those who want immediate gratification. It's also good as a summer iced tea aid. For more powerful results, use a dry red wine. Mendenhall recommends a zinfandel; "don't use a burgundy," he cautions. And stop by the Aspen store for a free taste, he says.

Conveniences: R **Credit Cards:** AE, MC, V **Shipping:** U.S.—R, X, UPS; A&H—R, X, UPS; C—R, X, UPS

ASPEN MULLING SPICES
Mulled Tea

---

1 quart orange juice
3 quarts tea
1 package spice mix

Mix well. Serve hot or cold.

Aspen Mulling Spices

Bickford Flavors

282 South Main Street, Akron, Ohio 44308

216·762·4666

*A*lmond. Anise. Apricot. Blueberry. Brandy. Butter. Sweet Cherry. Wild Cherry. Cherry with Pit. Maple. Maraschino. Mint. Peanut Butter. Tropical Fruit. Walnut. Wintergreen. Bickford's list of forty flavorings is a simple roster of choices. The labels and packaging are simple, too. Signs of an unpretentious company with a steady following. The concentrated liquids come in one-ounce rectangular-shaped glass jars, jars reminiscent of scale-model paints, complete with white metal screw-on caps. With a charm of their own, they'd fit well in stockings at Christmastime, as little additions to other presents and as surprises in unexpected places.

"Oils of natural herbs, vegetables, and fruits" printed on one side and "Contains no alcohol, sugar, salt" printed on the other are the only indications that Bickford's may be the unusual find it is. The biggest sellers—the dark and white vanillas—attract customers who must regulate their alcohol intake; the white vanilla also appeals to cooks, who use the colorless flavoring in white batters.

The one-ounce sizes sell for $1.59 each. The vanillas also come in two-ounce, four-ounce, eight-ounce, sixteen-ounce, and quart sizes (larger, too, if you're working in bulk) for $2.69, $4.89, $7.75, $12.50, and $19.95, respectively, with a flat $2.00 shipping charge.

Conveniences: none **Credit Cards:** MC, V **Shipping:** U.S.—R, UPS; A&H—R, UPS; C—R, UPS

The El Paso Chile Company™

100 Ruhlin Court, El Paso, Texas 79922

915·544·3434

*W*reaths and garlands are not just Christmas delights. El Paso's offerings make welcome additions to kitchens year-round. These hand-strung wreaths come in a variety of sizes. The traditional Whole Chile Circle measures twenty inches in diameter and sells for $33.00; the miniature version, at twelve inches, is only $23.00. They're nutritionally rich, too, as a good source of vitamin C. The longer, more slender Chile de Arbol also makes a fiery wreath ($28.00), as does the herbal array of chile, garlic, and bay ($30.00). Handsomely adorned, most with bows, these decorative edible treats are available natural or with a light coating of nongrease vegetable wax for a safe gloss shine.

El Paso's most popular item is their twenty-inch Chile Ristra. Other ristras—fancy and simple—are available. (See page 115 for catalog and store information.)

Conveniences: D, G, P, R **Credit Cards:** MC, V **Shipping:** U.S.—R, X, UPS; A&H—R; C—R, X, UPS

H.D. Cowan, Inc.

3813 Central Avenue, Doraville, Georgia 30340

404·451·4086

*T*he spice sections of most supermarkets are swimming with all-purpose seasoning salts and mixes, but if you read their labels carefully, you see that most of them contain chemicals, preservatives, high amounts of salt and fillers, and relatively little actual spice. H.D. Cowan's Fantastic Fixin's Seasoning Mix has a mere eight percent salt and contains none of the other undesirables—just a blend of pure spices. It's perfect for meat, fish, pork, raw or cooked vegetables, salads, and sauces, and is an excellent dry marinade and tenderizer. It comes in one-ounce, three-and-three-quarter-ounce, and five-ounce sizes at $1.00, $3.00, and $4.50, respectively.

H.D. Cowan offers two other excellent seasonings. First, Fantastic Fixin's Dry Barbeque Spice Mix, which was specially formulated as Cajun flavoring, but which also goes well in Italian and Mexican dishes. Fantastic Fixin's Dry Mustard Mix is delicious in sauces, condiments, dips, and spreads, and in egg salad, macaroni and cheese, slaw, bean and potato salad. The Barbeque Mix comes in a three-ounce size for $3.00, and the Mustard Mix is three-and-three-quarter ounces for $3.00. H.D. Cowan also offers a gift box of their three spices for $10.00, plus shipping. Minimum order is $10.00.

Conveniences: G, R, D **Credit Cards:** none **Shipping:** U.S.—UPS; A&H—R; C—R

Rathdowney Herbs Limited

3 River Street Bethel, Vermont 05032

802·234·5157

*W*hat is a Rathdowney? A town in Ireland, a family name, that in Gaelic means "Fort of the Downeys." Here in the New World, the appellation has also been affixed to the home-run business of Louise and Brendan Downey-Butler of Bethel, Vermont. The Downey-Butlers grow an amazing variety of herbs and spices on their parcel of land by the White River, and they have a number of small shops around the state from which they sell their fine fresh herbs. All are thoughtfully chosen and carefully harvested, and Louise has invented many extraordinary herbal mixtures and tested recipes in which to use them.

Among Rathdowney's homegrown specialties are Rosemary, Thyme, Calendula, Basil, Lavender, Dill, and Sweet Woodruff Prices on these flavorful organic herbs and spices are most reasonable, and Louise will be happy to send you a catalog from which to order.

Conveniences: P, R **Credit Cards:** MC, V, ($10.00) **Shipping:** U.S.—UPS; A&H—R; C—R

Select Origins Inc.

Box N, Southampton, New York 11968

516·288·1382

*I*f you love the wonderful things spices can do for food but find it bothersome to choose just the right combinations, let Select Origins do the blending for you—with a professional flair! Each of their six spice samplers has a culinary theme, such as Salad Blends, Cooks' Secrets, and In Praise of Pepper, each with four individual jars of specially blended herbs and spices. A spice booklet and recipes enclosed with each sampler provide copious cooking ideas that let you add the perfect balance of spices without guesswork.

Select Origins was founded in 1979 by Tom and Kristi Siplon, who kicked the corporate executive world and started the company in their apartment on New York's Upper West Side. From the start the Siplons' approach has been to find the best of each spice and herb at its source, buy in small select lots, and package quickly for ultimate freshness.

The Spice Samplers are $5.95 each, direct from Select Origins, and can also be found at Neiman-Marcus, Macy's, and Bloomingdale's. Select Origins also offers a Wild Mushroom Sampler featuring three premium-quality dried mushrooms: Japanese Shiitake, French Morels, and Italian Porcini. It weighs nine ounces and costs $9.00.

Conveniences: G, R, P, D **Credit Cards:** AE, MC ($15.00), V **Shipping:** U.S.—R, UPS

Select Origins Inc.

60

Snow White and Rose Red

P.O. Box 275, Springville, Utah 84663

801·489·7982

*H*ere's an exciting idea for the modern American baker—dry powdered vanilla, a unique and delicious form of vanilla recently perfected by Trudy Owens of Springville, Utah. Dry vanilla is relatively new to America, but Europe's finest bakeries have used it for years, says Chef Trudy.

The great thing about Snow White and Rose Red Powdered Vanilla is that its rich, pure vanilla flavor stays in the baking, instead of baking out like alcohol-based vanillas.

The company's packaging won an award at the fourth International Gourmet Food & Wine Show, so it makes an excellent gift for friends who like to bake.

Snow White and Rose Red is available in a three-quarter-ounce pouch (equals three ounces liquid) or three-ounce canister (equals twelve ounces liquid), at $2.00 and $5.00, respectively. There is no minimum order.

Conveniences: P **Credit Cards:** MC, V **Shipping:** U.S.—R

Snow White and Rose Red   Spicehampton Limited

Spicehampton Limited

425 Riverside Drive, Penthouse Two, New York, New York 10025

212·316·6561

*C*ooking with herbs and spices in place of salt is a good idea, but few cooks have the ability to combine just the right amounts of parsley, tarragon, marjoram, mustard, basil, oregano, pepper, and especially garlic and onion. Spicehampton Limited, a young company out of New York City's Upper West Side, has formulated six varieties of seasonings that eliminate the need for a complete rack of spices, that will elevate your cooking to the gourmet level, yet which have no salt, sugar, MSG, or preservatives. The set includes seasonings for fish, poultry, meat, pasta, vegetables, and dips, and each jar comes with two recipes.

Each of the seasonings contains several herbs and spices, mixed and balanced to perfection. The Seasoning for Seafood, for example, contains basil, marjoram, ginger, thyme, parsley, sage, pepper, ground bay leaves, savory, onion, and garlic. No one herb or spice overpowers the others, and the flavor is superb.

Spicehampton has no minimum order on their seasonings. You can order any individual 1.5-ounce jar at $2.00 each, or they offer attractive wicker gift baskets of three, four, or six jars at $6.50, $8.25, and $12.50, respectively.

Conveniences: G, R **Credit Cards:** none **Shipping:** U.S.—UPS; A&H—R; C—R, UPS

Tsang and Ma

Tsang and Ma

P.O. Box 294, Belmont, California 94002

415·595·2270

*C*ook up a pot of rice, slice a few of your favorite vegetables, heat up the wok, and then let Tsang and Ma turn your stir-fry into an exotic regional gourmet experience. Just add any one of the five special spice mixtures in their Five Exotic Regional Experiences pack, and your meal is distinctly transformed. The seasoning set includes Szechuan Hot & Sour, Peking Mongolian Fire, Polynesia Lemon Luau, Indo-China Coconut Curry, and Japan Teriyaki.
Tsang and Ma's Gourmet Seasoning set makes an excellent gift for lovers of Oriental cuisine, as it comes gift-wrapped and includes great, easy recipes for such dishes as Aluau Mushroom and Zucchini, Teriyaki Crispy Chicken, and Hot and Sour Egg Flower Soup. The set sells for $10.50.

Conveniences: R, P, D, G **Credit Cards:** MC, V **Shipping:** U.S.—UPS; A&H—R, UPS; C—R, UPS

United Society of Shakers

Sabbathday Lake, Poland Spring, Maine 04274

207·926·4597

*T*rue to the aesthetic of Shaker simplicity, the herbs and teas of Sabbathday Lake are packaged in plain reusable slipcover tins with blue and red print on old-fashioned pale yellow or white labels. The aromas from within these tins may very well hark back to former times; these are the same herbs and teas that were used when the Shakers were in their heyday. The United Society of Shakers has maintained an Herb Department continuously since 1799. Today, the last active Shaker community, at Sabbathday Lake, markets fifty-four varieties of herbal teas and culinary herbs; many of the herbs continue to be cultivated on the two-thousand-acre farm.
The prices range from $1.50 to just over $4.00 for the Marshmallow Root Tea. Write to the address above for the current price list. A gift box of Basil, Mint, Sweet Cicely, and Tarragon vinegars makes another attractive gift; the package comes with recipes and suggested uses ($8.50 plus postage). And at Christmastime the community offers an Alfred Fruitcake; again, write for details.

Conveniences: G, H, P, R **Credit Cards:** none **Shipping:** U.S.—UPS; A&H—UPS; C—UPS

JOHN WILLIAM LUND

CHAPTER EIGHT

Oils, Vinegars and Dressings

Calvert Cedar Street Inc.

3 South Fourth Street, Wilmington, North Carolina 28401

919·763·9433

*L*ook carefully at the Calvert label; the house in print really is the home of the creator of these fine products. The care and imagination that lead to a detail like that also lead to a fine line of quality mustards and salad dressings. Rita Calvert's Cedar Street Cafe in Santa Cruz, California, was the original home of these exceptionally fine products, although the company now hails from the North Carolina coast.

The modern classic—Bumpy Beer Mustard—gets its name from the mix of crunchy, bumpy poppy, yellow, and black mustard seeds. The mustards come in six flavors: Bumpy Beer, Dill, Chive, Basil, Garlic, and a smooth-textured, sweet, hot Original Style—each for $3.95 for an eight-ounce jar.

Bumpy Beer Mustard begat a personal favorite—Bumpy Beer Salad Dressing, which comes in pleasing-to-look-at eight-ounce antique-style bottles. The Pecan Vinaigrette and Shallot Vermouth Vinaigrette are also pretty special and certainly unique. These, too, sell for $3.95 for eight ounces.

College students or others away from home will enjoy receiving the Carolina Care Package, a jar each of the two Bumpy Beer products and Southern Bourbon Sweets; it's all tidily contained in a split-wood peach basket bedded with natural straw. A blue-plaid ribbon and note card complete the package ($12.95).

Plan early, for all holiday orders must be in by mid-November.

Conveniences: G, H, P, R **Credit Cards:** none **Shipping:** U.S.—UPS; A&H—R; C—UPS

Calvert Cedar Street Inc.

Cuisine Perel

P.O. Box 1064, Tiburon, California 94920

415·435·1282

Sylvia Perel came to northern California from her native Argentina with the know-how of a fine saucière. She and her husband Leonardo learned of the excellent wines of the Napa, Monterey, and Sonoma areas, and the connection was obvious. Sylvia could make great sauces without fine wines, but a good cook always accepts the help of a regional specialty. So Perel, being better than good, not only used California wines in her dressings and sauces, she based her entire line of sauces and dressings on the wines. And the results are astounding.

Cuisine Perel offers five wine-based salad dressings, including Garlic-Dill Sauterne, Lemon Chardonnay, Champagne Mustard, Goat Cheese Riesling, and Zinfandel Tomato. One newspaper food editor called the Lemon Chardonnay dressing "the best salad dressing in the world." Another pointed to the Champagne Mustard—but they are all of the highest order, rich in such ingredients as pure egg yolks and without artificial flavors, preservatives, colorants, salt, sugar, or MSG. Perel's dressings also go excellently on other foods besides salads. The Zinfandel Tomato, for example, is perfect on ribs and pasta, while the Garlic-Dill Sauterne enlivens chicken and vegetables. All dressings come in attractive 12.7-ounce bottles and cost $4.00 each, plus shipping. They are also available at Neiman-Marcus, Gimbel's, Macy's, and I. Magnin.

Conveniences: R, D **Credit Cards:** none **Shipping:** U.S.—UPS; A&H—X; C—UPS

CALVERT'S CEDAR STREET

Beef Marinade: ⅔ cup dry red wine; 2 tablespoons fresh lemon juice; ½ cup olive oil; 2 tablespoons Calvert's Basil Mustard; 2 cloves fresh garlic, minced; 2 anchovy filets, minced; 1 tablespoon fresh thyme leaves or 1 teaspoon dried thyme; salt and freshly ground black pepper, to taste; 4 pounds beef roast or steaks.

Pork Marinade: Juice of 2 fresh oranges plus 1 tablespoon grated orange rind; ⅔ cup dry vermouth; ½ cup olive oil; 2 tablespoons soy sauce; 2 tablespoons Calvert's Chive Mustard; 1 bay leaf; 2 cloves fresh garlic, pressed; 3–4 pounds pork.

Chicken Marinade: ¼ cup olive oil, ½ cup fresh lemon juice, 1 tablespoon Calvert's Garlic Mustard, ¼ cup fresh snipped dill or 2 teaspoons dried dill weed, ¼ teaspoon salt, freshly ground black pepper, 3½ pounds whole or cut up chicken.

CALVERT'S CEDAR STREET
Sunchoke Salad

1 sunchoke or Jerusalem artichoke, scrubbed and sliced very thinly
1 bunch scallions, cleaned and chopped
2 fresh tomatoes, cut into ½-inch dices
1 bunch fresh parsley, chopped fine
1 tablespoon fresh lemon juice
Calvert Cedar Street Shallot Vermouth Vinaigrette
Salt to taste

Toss all ingredients together and let marinate at least 2 hours or overnight. Makes six servings.

CUISINE PEREL
Satay Sticks

Cut beef, pork, or chicken into thin strips. Combine crushed fresh garlic, lemon juice, salad oil, and white wine. Cover meat strips and marinate 30–60 minutes. Thread on skewers and barbecue quickly over mesquite charcoal or oven broiler. Pour Hot Thai Peanut Dressing over Satay Sticks before serving.

CUISINE PEREL
Roasted Peppers Salad

Heat red bell peppers in a preheated 450°F oven until skins are black and peppers are soft. Cool, peel skin, and slice in fine julienne, discarding stems and seeds. You can also heat over an open flame. Add artichoke hearts, crumbled feta cheese, black olives, fresh mushrooms, and green onions. Refrigerate to mingle flavors. Serve with Goat Cheese & Herbs Riesling Dressing over crisp greens. Arugula is a peppery addition to this salad, if you can find it. Sesame seeds will also make the salad special.

Duggan's Ingredients

1365 Interior Street #A, Eugene, Oregon 97402

503·343·8697

*A*t first glance, Duggan's Ingredients will beckon to you. You might not *really* want that salad dressing, seasoned oil, or flavored vinegar, but it's out of your hands. Or, rather, the beautifully designed bottles will be in your hands. You can see the ingredients: the marjoram, the garlic, the boysenberries. The mint or the rosemary and cloves in the cider vinegar. The lemon thyme and seeds in the olive oil.

Duggan Peak creates something extraordinary with her ingredients; and she transforms the already extraordinary into a unique treasure with the help of Santo, an artist from the Northwest who hand-paints and stencils each tongue-and-groove wooden gift box, using dark-hued pastels. "Each box is different, because they vary with Santo's moods," says Robert Peak, Duggan's husband, "and he's never in a bad mood."

The talent in this combination far exceeds the norm. Duggan lent her touch to menus at the River Cafe and the American Bar and Grill in New York and at Michael's in California. She can enter your kitchen through mail order or department stores such as Neiman-Marcus and Macy's. Write, call, or run to the nearest outlet for the full list of Duggan's temptingly described products. The 12.7-ounce bottles of vinegar sell for between $4.50 and $5.00; the same size oils run for about $7.00; and her unique salad dressings—Italian-Zap, Duggan's Own, and Poppy Perfect—are $6.00. Write for the current prices of the three-bottle and nine-bottle gift boxes; you'll have your choice of natural, blue, pink, green, or holiday green for the boxes. Order as early as you can for Christmas.

Conveniences: D, G **Credit Cards:** AE, MC, V **Shipping:** U.S.—R, X, UPS; A&H—R, X, UPS; C—R, X, UPS

Duggan's Ingredients

Gourmet Foods, Inc.

P.O. Box 419, Knoxville, Tennessee 37901-0419

615·970·2982

*T*he Peppervine family of sauces was introduced at the thirty-first Annual International Fancy Food and Confection Show, July 14-17, 1985. A relative newcomer to the gourmet market, these four sauces present a new twist to an old standby. The Fancy Worcestershire Sauce adds sherry wine and Cajun peppers to the traditional vinegar-spice blend. It adds a good dash of spice to stir-fries and warm salads. The Fancy Blend Spicy Pepper Sauce's ingredients blend in a secret combination that makes a superb accompaniment for meats and seafoods and perks up soups, dips, and Bloody Marys. Try the Fancy Hot Pepper Sauce in your Bloody Mary too—or use it on chili, steamed eggs, and poached fish. The cayenne peppers will go straight to your head. The zesty Gourmet Beef and Burger Sauce is a bit more distinctive than most, with a pungent, delicious finesse of anchovies and hot red pepper.

The sauces come in five-ounce bottles, twelve to a case ($12.00).

Conveniences: G **Credit Cards:** MC, V, ($15.00) **Shipping:** U.S.—UPS; A—R; H—R, UPS; C—R

Gourmet Foods, Inc.

Joyce Chen Products, Inc.

411 Waverley Oaks Road, Waltham, Massachusetts 02154

617·894·9020

Cooking fads do come and go now, almost as surely as fashion trends. What remains becomes a modern classic: chili, quiche, and now stir-fries, a generic term for a delicious Chinese preparation. Quick and simple, stir-frying eases the schedules of harried cooks; and using Joyce Chen's sauces makes the task almost effortless. These one-step cooking sauces are all you need besides the fish, meat, or vegetables (for thicker sauces, Joyce Chen recommends adding a small amount of cornstarch) for a good home-cooked Chinese meal.

The Zesty Spice Stir-Fry Sauce, for instance, includes soy sauce, sugar syrup, cider vinegar, sherry, fermented black soybeans, garlic, and spices—a traditional mix of acid, sweet, and piquant flavorings. The Szechuan Stir-Fry Sauce, a rich and savory addition to your wok or frying pan, recalls the cuisine of Imperial China. Less classic but just as good are the Lemon Spice and Orange Spice Stir-Fry Sauces. All are available in ten-ounce bottles for approximately $3.50. You can order a twelve-bottle stir-fry assortment from the company or smaller amounts through a number of catalogs: Adam York, Colonial Garden Kitchen, Comfortably Yours, the Wooden Spoon, and Zabar's. Burdine's, Filene's, Macy's, Sherman's, and a number of other United States and Canadian department stores carry the products.

Keep an eye out, too, for Joyce Chen's Sushi Food Kit, complete with *nori* (seaweed), sushi rice, seasoning for the rice, wasabi (a hot green horseradish), and pickled ginger. The kit sells for approximately $11.95.

Conveniences: D, G, P, R **Credit Cards:** none **Shipping:** U.S.—UPS; A&H—UPS; C—UPS

Joyce Chen is no ordinary entrepreneur. Restaurateur, lecturer, consultant, she is renowned as an international authority on Chinese cooking. Television viewers may recognize her as the host of a PBS cooking show and the documentary "Joyce Chen's China." Her cookbook, a modern classic, has won accolades from gourmets as well as from members of the medical community. Dr. Paul Dudley White wrote in the foreword: "Joyce Chen's recipes are a delight to the gourmet . . . they represent Chinese cooking at its best . . . and they are good for the health." The same can be said of her products (see above).

Beyond the kitchen, Ms. Chen served in 1983 as Boston's City Ambassador to its sister city Hang Zhou and, more recently, was honored with an invitation to attend a White House state reception for Chinese Premier Zhao Ziyang. And John Kenneth Galbraith, the noted economist and former U.S. Ambassador to India, extends the compliments and has said that "she combines scholarship and political sense with damn good food."

A director of the Fulbright Scholarship Committee and one of the select to be listed in *Who's Who of the World,* Joyce Chen brings an exceptional sense of quality and intelligence to the kitchen—and the world.

JOYCE CHEN
Mandarin Orange Spice Beef

1 pound boneless beef steak—flank is best
4 tablespoons Orange Spice Stir Fry Sauce
1 tablespoon cornstarch
3 tablespoons cooking oil
1 (11-ounce) can mandarin oranges, drained

Cut 2-inch-wide beef strips across the grain into ¼-inch slices. Combine meat with Orange Spice Sauce and cornstarch. Set aside. Heat oil in wok or skillet over medium-high heat. Add well-mixed beef and stir constantly until almost done, about 3–4 minutes. Add 1–3 tablespoons water as needed to help prevent meat from sticking to pan.

Add drained mandarin orange sections to meat and stir gently. Serve hot.

Judyth's Mountain Inc.

1737 Lorenzen Drive, San Jose, California 95124

408·264·3330

Judyth's Mountain is on a constant quest for new gourmet food combinations, and it has thus developed one of America's most unusual, varied, and intriguing product lines and has been a consistent award winner at international fancy-food competitions.

In 1985 Judyth's Mountain introduced their barrel-aged Chardonnay Wine Vinegar, an extraordinary vinegar that adds depth and character to salad dressings and savory entrees alike. This came after their Aceto California Red Wine Vinegar, which is itself a winner.

Another new product in 1985 was Judyth's Mountain Coffee Jelly, a jelly so delicious, it makes croissants beg the question, "Where have you been all my life?" Judyth's Mountain didn't stop with plain coffee flavor. No, you have a choice of Coffee Almond, Coffee Orange, and Coffee Chocolate, all of which are made with real French Roast coffee.

Judyth's Mountain also features a variety of flavorful pasta sauces, such as Cream Garlic Sauce and excellent Herb Oils. While you can't order directly from Judyth's Mountain unless you order by the case, its products are found in many large department stores, including Macy's, I. Magnin, Neiman-Marcus, Dayton's, Davison's, and others.

Conveniences: R, G, D **Credit Cards:** none **Shipping:** U.S.—UPS (only if ordered by the case)

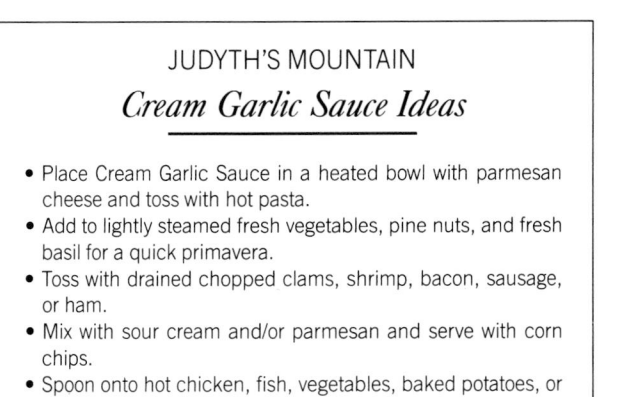

JUDYTH'S MOUNTAIN

Cream Garlic Sauce Ideas

- Place Cream Garlic Sauce in a heated bowl with parmesan cheese and toss with hot pasta.
- Add to lightly steamed fresh vegetables, pine nuts, and fresh basil for a quick primavera.
- Toss with drained chopped clams, shrimp, bacon, sausage, or ham.
- Mix with sour cream and/or parmesan and serve with corn chips.
- Spoon onto hot chicken, fish, vegetables, baked potatoes, or creamed soups.
- Grill with cheese on french bread.

Market Square Food Company

1642 Richfield, Highland Park, Illinois 60035

312·831·2228 or 1·800·232·2299

Anne and David Lockhart, owners and managers of Market Square Food Company, have earned their company an excellent reputation by faithfully and proudly offering a selected array of the finest American-grown food products. Among their personal favorites in the company's growing and various gourmet product lines (see page 115 for others) are an assortment of premium-quality oils and wine vinegars.

Market Square has two fine wine vinegars—Chardonnay and Cabernet. Both are made from high-quality California wines and are oak-barrel-aged for a remarkable full-bodied flavor. They come in a twenty-four-ounce flip-top shaker reusable bottle for $5.00 or in a twelve-ounce bottle at $3.50. These excellent vinegars will do wonders for salads or cooked dishes. Market Square's gourmet oils include 100 percent pure, cold-pressed Peanut Oil, Sunflower Oil, and Extra Virgin California Olive Oil. Each of the oils has its own distinct character and delicious flavor. The Olive Oil sells for $8.00 for twenty-four ounces or $4.75 for twelve ounces, and the other oils are $5.00 for twenty-four ounces and $3.50 for twelve ounces. They are also available at Bloomingdale's, Macy's, B. Altman, and Marshall Fields.

Conveniences: D, G, R **Credit Cards:** MC, V, ($15.00) **Shipping:** U.S.—UPS; A&H—UPS; C—UPS

Paula's California Herb Vinegars and Premium Oils

SWEET ADELAIDE ENTERPRISES INC.
3457-A South La Cienega Boulevard, Los Angeles, California 90016
213•559•6196

*P*aula's California herb vinegars glow with subtle hues: autumnal ambers, translucent roses, and a pale woody green. The labels carry an elegant simplicity, reminders of the bookmarks she once used for that purpose. The bottles do not conjure up old-world opulence; rather, they bring to mind the studied freshness of modern design. The vinegars themselves are equal metaphors—complex yet simple.

Paula Fishman-Savett chooses fine white, cider, and wine vinegars to combine with her garden-fresh herbs. She no longer personally delivers the results in a hand-carried basket, but her products do deliver good taste. For instance, the Raspberry Royale blends white wine vinegar, raspberry syrup, raspberry liqueur, and lavender flower; it is not simply raspberry vinegar.

The complete line includes five more vinegars and the more recent additions—an unrefined 100 percent natural olive oil and a premium pecan oil.

Although they are not available in single bottles, you can buy the two dozen minimum and distribute the booty to friends. A case of twelve for the Raspberry Royale costs $30.25; a mixed case of six flavors, $31.25; and the rest, $30.25. Shoppers can also find them at some Neiman-Marcus, Macy's, and Marshall Fields department stores.

Conveniences: D, R **Credit Cards:** none **Shipping:** U.S.—UPS and common carrier; A&H—overseas carrier; C—UPS

Market Square Food Company

Paula's California Herb Vinegars and Premium Oils

BRIAN LEATART

CHAPTER NINE

Charcuterie and Other Meats

Commonwealth Enterprises Limited

P.O. Box 49, Mongaup Valley, New York 12762

914·583·6630

Cook it quickly and it becomes a jewel to adorn any dish—it's fresh foie gras from the United States of America. Since force-feeding geese and ducks is illegal in the U.S., as is importing the exquisite substance fresh, father-and-son entrepreneurs Rubin and Howard Josephs came up with a method to fatten their fowl legally and without chemicals or hormones. The result is a delicacy—expensive but cheaper than its precooked, canned, imported counterpart—that is being served in some of the leading hotels and restaurants of the country. (The method, by the way, is a well-kept secret.) Judith Hill, editor of *The Cook's Magazine,* describes these fatted livers with a panache worth repeating: "Foie gras is redundantly good, even more suave, satiny, and subtle than necessary to be exquisitely rich and delicious." Texture comes to the fore time and time again: "silky," "like velvet," "indescribably smooth," say others with distinguishing palates. The Moulard Duck Foie Gras, weighing one and a quarter pounds in its package, sells for $60.00, including shipping. .Request recipes when ordering, and you'll be guided to some rare treats. The first of December is the holiday deadline.

Conveniences: H, P, R **Credit Cards:** none **Shipping:** U.S.—UPS; A&H—UPS

S. Wallace Edwards & Sons, Inc.

Box 25, Surry, Virginia 23883

804·294·3121 *or* 1·800·222·4267

Premium-quality hickory-smoked Virginia hams, bacon, and sausage are the specialty of this sixty-year-old family company. Only the finest hams are selected, and each is hand-rubbed with a special dry cure, smoked for days over a cool hickory fire, then aged for several months. The result is a lovely mahogany-colored ham with a rich hickory flavor that's unbeatable.

S. Wallace Edwards & Sons got started in 1926, when a young Virginia ferryboat captain named S. Wallace Edwards first served a ham sandwich to one of his passengers. The ham had been cured on his family farm. So quickly did demand grow that the young captain began curing and selling the smoked delicacy on a full-time basis. Now, Edwards' son and grandson run the business, using the captain's same tested methods.

S. Wallace Edwards & Sons products are available at Bloomingdale's, Marshall Fields, Neiman-Marcus, and by direct mail. A five-pound box of Virginia Smoked Sausage sells for $18.75, or you can order a two-pound cloth gift bag for $11.60. Country-style Virginia Smoked Bacon comes in four- to six-pound half-slabs for $3.79 a pound, and arrives packed in Edwards' traditional burlap bag. Edwards' Hickory-Smoked Virginia Hams, bone-in, weigh nine to eleven pounds and cost $5.25 a pound. It arrives at your door ready to slice and serve for a buffet party, formal dinner, or family sandwiches.

Conveniences: G, R, P, H, D **Credit Cards:** AE, MC, V **Shipping:** U.S.—UPS; A&H—R

Lawrence's Smoke House

Rte. 30, RR#1 Box 28, Newfane, Vermont 05345
802·365·7751

*L*awrence's is the only smokehouse we found that smokes exclusively with corncobs, maintaining the tradition of the Native American Indians of "New England," who were smoking with corncob when the Colonists arrived. The rich smokey flavor produced by this process is utterly unique and decidedly delicious. Hot or cold, the ham makes an excellent main course, or slice it thinly for simple yet sophisticated hors d'oeuvres. The cob-smoked slab bacon adds an unforgettable accent to the breakfast meal.

The Traditional Corn Cob Smoked Ham with Bone comes in a five- to six-pound half-ham size for about $38.00 or a nine- to ten-pound whole ham for about $57.00. For grandest fetes, ham sizes go all the way up to twenty pounds. A half-slab of Corn Cob Smoked Bacon weighs four to four-and-a-half pounds and sells for about $21.00. For gourmands, Lawrence's also offers a supreme Canadian Style Boneless Loin Bacon: one-half loin (two to two-and-a-half pounds) for $25.00; whole (five to six pounds) at $51.00.

Conveniences: G, R, P, H **Credit Cards:** MC, V ($25.00) **Shipping:** U.S.—R, UPS, UPS Air

S. Wallace Edwards & Sons, Inc.

Les Trois Petits Cochons, Inc.

c/o BALDUCCI'S
424 Avenue of the Americas, New York, New York 10011
1·800·228·2028, ext. 72
212·673·2600

*A*lthough this wonderfully elegant line of pâtés and mousses is not available by mail order through the company, LTPC does sell their scrumptious goods through a number of catalogs: The Neiman-Marcus Christmas Catalogue, Marshall Fields Christmas and Gourmet Gift Catalogues, Pfaelzer Bros. Catalog, Balducci's Mail Order Catalogue, and Culpeper Fine Provisions, Ltd. Also, Neiman-Marcus, Woodward & Lothrop, Wanamaker's, Davison's, Robinson's, and Youncker's are only a few of the department stores across the country that stock LTPC's pâtés.

The newest addition to the line—the Mousse Royale, a goose-liver mousse flavored with sauterne and cèpes—may very well be the best (at least, to our tastes!): Light, fluffy, and deliciously decadent, it teases the palate with a certain assurance that is lacking in many mousses. Others in the LTPC family include a tasty, more traditional Pâté Forestier (wild-mushroom pâté), a Mousse Truffle (a luxurious chicken-liver and truffle pâté with sherry and Pineau des Charente), and a hearty Canard a l'Orange (duck pâté with pistachios and orange).

The catalogs' individual and gift packages range from $12.00 to $60.00, plus shipping. As always when ordering perishables by mail, check for current selections and prices.

Conveniences: D, R **Credit Cards:** AE, MC, V, ($15.00) **Shipping:** U.S.—Federal Express; A&H—Federal Express

---

LES TROIS PETITS COCHONS, INC.
Pâté serving suggestions

A Classic First Course Serve one slice of pâté the way the French do—to begin everything from a casual lunch to an elegant dinner. Garnish it with a lettuce leaf and cornichons, and serve with mustard, french bread, and red wine.

Strictly Vegetarian Serve two styles of vegetable pâté on a luncheon plate. Garnish with parsley, watercress, bean sprouts, radishes, and cherry tomatoes. May be served with watercress sauce or tomato coulis. Delicious served warm.

Easy Canapés Press softened mousse into pastry bag and decorate crackers or toast points. Thin slices of coarse pâtés may be sliced to fit crackers or toast points. Garnish with olives and cornichons.

Les Trois Petits Cochons, Inc.

McArthur's Smokehouse, Inc.

Main Street, Millerton, New York 12546

518·789·4425

*P*lan for McArthur's smoked boneless breast of chicken to arrive on a hot night, a night that makes you cringe to think of turning on your oven. You'll appreciate the package all the more. McArthur's American Cornucopia includes foods that reflect the character and tradition of American cuisine. The New England cured hickory-smoked hams are less salty and dry than their southern counterparts. Baked, scored, and glazed, they're ready for the table. The slab- and Canadian-style bacon are cured in molasses and salt water—like the hams—before they're soaked in fresh water to remove the excess salt. The smoked fowl are equally good: succulent and robust.

We didn't have a chance to try the smoked fish, but if the salmons, tuna, and mackerel fall within the same range of quality, they're sure to be good.

Gift assortments can be packed in a serviceable package or a nice-looking wooden box (add $5.00 for the box); there are many selections from which to choose, or you can "invent" your own gift sampler. Prices for all McArthur's products would be too numerous to list here, but a few examples are the smoked game hen ($7.95 for one pound), half ham ($24.95 for average five pounds), smoked yellowfin tuna ($32.50 for two-and-a-half-pound side), and slab Canadian-style bacon ($15.75 for two pounds). Holiday orders should be in by December 9.

Conveniences: G, H, P **Credit Cards:** AE, MC, V **Shipping:** U.S.—UPS

Meadow Farms Country Smokehouse

P.O. Box 1387, 2345 North Sierra Highway, Bishop, California 93514

619·873·5311

*R*oi Ballard simply has the best beef jerky we've come across; peppery and pliant, the Top Sirloin Slab Jerky is well worth the $30.00-a-pound price.

The Mahogany Smoked Meats of Meadow Farms are smoked with Sierra Nevada real mountain mahogany, an aromatic wood so dense that it will not float in water. Collected only after it has fallen, the wood logs by that time are about 300 years old. The aged mahogany imparts a very special flavor to the meats, a distinct taste as different from hickory as hickory is from mesquite. The process is unique to Meadow Farms. In fact, Roi Ballard challenges all new customers to grill three strips of his bacon next to three strips of other mail-order bacon. He's convinced "you'll be sending for my bacon again real fast."

The bacon and ham rival the beef jerky for flavor; the cooking meat sends forth a heady smell, smoky but sweet. Sliced bacon sells for $8.00 for a two-pound package (the minimum); the half slab bacon is $15.00 for approximately four to five pounds, unsliced. Whole slab bacon weighs in at eight to ten pounds and sells for $33.00. Write for details on the hams, Canadian bacon, pork chops, and gift boxes.

Conveniences: G, H, P, R **Credit Cards:** MC, V **Shipping:** U.S.—X, UPS; A&H—X, UPS

Michel's Magnifique

34 North Moore Street, New York, New York 10013

212·431·1070

*M*ichel's Magnifique is one of the select few companies in North America to offer fine, sophisticated charcuterie. The small plant is headed by Ken Blanchette, a food technologist, nutritionist, caterer, and chef, known for his innovative blendings of herbs, spices, and liqueurs with fresh meats. He pioneered the lighter-style pâtés that hosts and hostesses are turning to today.

Specialties here include the mixed-vegetable pâté and the rabbit pâté with calvados. The whole larder contains over twenty pâtés, mousses, saucissons, and gallantines as well as a collection of fresh-fruit relishes.

The prices for the pâtés, packed in an attractive beribboned basket (one-pound), range from $21.50 to $22.60. Send in your holiday orders at least one week ahead of the requested delivery date, if not sooner. And if you'd rather, you can order Michel's Magnifique through the Zabar's or Austin Market catalogs.

Conveniences: G, H, P **Credit Cards:** none **Shipping:** U.S.—UPS; A&H—X, UPS; C—X, UPS

Michel's Magnifique

The Peanut Patch

P.O. Box 186, Courtland, Virginia 23837

804·653·2028

Sure, Southampton County, Virginia, is the world's largest peanut-producing county, but it's also the state's largest pork-producing county, which itself ain't exactly peanuts. So, having mastered the little-known art of gourmet peanut cookery, the Peanut Patch got into hams—smoked ones—and they got *them* down, too.

The Peanut Patch's pork prize is called the Old Virginia Ham. It's an uncooked country-cured and smoked long shank, fourteen to eighteen pounds, that's been aged for one full year. It's an excellently flavored, no-nonsense gourmet-quality ham that sells at a very reasonable $3.25 a pound. The Southampton Ham Short Shank is also uncooked, cured, and smoked, but is aged three to six months and weighs twelve to fifteen pounds. It costs about $2.25 a pound. The Southampton Country Cured Picnic Shoulder (five to eight pounds) goes for about $2.15 a pound. Southampton Country Cured Slab Bacon weighs two to three pounds and is $2.50 a pound. Shipping charges are added to all orders according to weight and destination. The Peanut Patch accepts phone orders Monday through Saturday, from 9:30 to 5:00, and Sunday from 2:00 to 5:00.

Conveniences: G, P, R **Credit Cards:** AE, MC, V **Shipping:** U.S.—UPS; A&H—R; C—R, UPS

Santa Barbara Olive Company, Inc.

P.O. Box 3825, Santa Barbara, California 93105

805·683·1932

One taste of these flavorful beauties and the word "olive" will take on new meaning. Each Santa Barbara Olive Company olive is special—a plump thing of beauty first, but more important, a burst of rich, subtle flavor that puts canned olives to shame.

Santa Barbara Olive Company starts by selecting only the very finest organically grown, tree-ripened olives from the beautiful hillside groves surrounding Santa Barbara. The olives are then cured in a variety of fine solutions that include such ingredients as California red wine, fresh garlic, and quality vermouth. Craig Makela, president and owner of the Santa Barbara Olive Company, is a fifth generation Santa Barbaran—not an easy thing to find—who knows his olives and keeps his standards high.

Santa Barbara Olive Company's 100 percent cold-pressed, unrefined Extra Virgin Olive Oil has been used and lauded by such chefs as Michael Hutchings, Wolfgang Puck, and Julia Child.

Santa Barbara Olive Company offers fourteen varieties of spiced and stuffed olives, including Wine Cured, Country Style, Italian, Garlic, Greek Black, Jalapeño Stuffed, and a special Martini Olive, stuffed with fat slices of pimiento. They come in a handsome gift pack that includes four different ten-ounce jars of spiced gourmet olives and a six-ounce bottle of Extra Virgin Olive Oil, for $19.95. The Olive Oil is offered in six-ounce bottles at $3.00 each, with a minimum order of twelve bottles. Or it comes in attractive 25.4-ounce wine bottles at $9.00 a bottle, six bottle minimum. Buy it by the gallon too—$24.00 a gallon, three gallon minimum.

Conveniences: G, R, P, D **Credit Cards:** MC, V **Shipping:** U.S.—R, X, UPS; A&H—R; C—R

Santa Barbara Olive Company, Inc.

Sunny Meadows Inc.

P.O. Box 437, Baird Road, Stowe, Vermont 05672

802·253·4641

Sunny Meadows brings a French accent to Vermont—with substantial American-made pâtés. Satisfyingly fresh-tasting, these Vermont Country Delicacies make wonderful summer or autumn meals served simply with cornichons, a good, fresh bread, and a bottle of red wine. Besides the standard Pâté de Campagne and Pâté with Green Peppercorns, Peter Koeck, the man behind the pâtés at Sunny Meadows, offers an unusual Spring Lamb Pâté and a full, well-rounded Pâté with Wild Mushrooms.

The three-and-a-half-pound loaves run about $6.25 to $7.25 a pound, but check for current prices and selections before ordering. New Yorkers have the added privilege of being able to shop for Koeck's pâtés at Bloomingdale's and Macy's.

Conveniences: D, G, P, R **Credit Cards:** AE, MC, V **Shipping:** U.S.—UPS; A&H—UPS; C—UPS

SUNNY MEADOWS INC.
Blueberry Tart with Melon Jelly Glaze

PASTRY:
1 cup flour
½ cup sweet butter
2 tablespoons powdered sugar

Put all ingredients into a food processor fitted with a metal blade. Process until mixture resembles cornmeal. Pour into a 9-inch tart pan with a removable bottom. Press firmly onto bottom and sides. Bake in preheated oven at 425°F for 10–12 minutes. Cool, remove from pan.

FILLING:
Fresh blueberries
1 jar Sunny Meadow Melon Jelly
Finely chopped walnuts

Arrange blueberries in tart shell. Melt jelly over low heat and pour over blueberries. Try not to get jelly on tart shell. Sprinkle finely chopped walnuts around the edge.

Sunny Meadows Inc.

SUNNY MEADOWS INC.
Cold Salmon with Cucumber Jelly and Sour Cream

Cold poached salmon
Parsley
Sunny Meadow Cucumber Jelly
Sour cream

Arrange salmon on a serving platter. Garnish with fresh parsley. Mix Cucumber Jelly with sour cream to taste. Serve a little on each plate with salmon.

Sunny Meadows

Peter Koeck of Stowe, Vermont, was once described in a newspaper article as "an engineer by education and a ski instructor by desire," but it is cooking that has turned Koeck's head and made him the entrepreneur he has become. Sunny Meadows produces fine pâtés and intriguing maple goodies: a dessert sauce, a tangy mustard, and a tangy salad dressing. He takes pride in bringing Vermont products into homes throughout North America. And as every person has a story, so has Peter Koeck. This one begins in Washington, D.C., where he went to get federal approval for his label.

"When I told the clerk at the front desk my name and where I was from," Koeck recalls, "she looked at me and asked what country Vermont was in. I thought she must be pulling my leg, but she wasn't.

"Finally," he continues, "the label made it to the appropriate person who then decided it wouldn't do because it advertised Sunny Meadow products as Vermont Country Delicacies." Because the clerk didn't think Stowe was in the country, the label was judged to be misleading. Koeck had to describe the landscape and the grazing animals before he convinced the clerk of Stowe's pastoral charms.

CHAPTER TEN

Cheeses

GUY BOUCHET (KIM FREEMAN, stylist)

Crowley Cheese Factory

Healdville, Vermont 05758

802·259·2340

*T*hey call this the cheese that made Vermont cheese famous, and with good reason. Crowley Cheese has been made since 1882 in the oldest continuously operated cheese factory in the United States, now designated a National Historic Place. The cheese here is still made by hand in exactly the same way used by its originator, Winfield Crowley, and has thereby retained its supremely moist texture and subtle cheddar/Colby character throughout the decades. It has been enjoyed by presidents, Supreme Court justices, and a select, dedicated few who knew where to find it.

In judging a competition among American cheeses, Mimi Sheraton, former food critic of the *New York Times,* wrote, "My favorite was far and away Crowley Cheese, technically a Colby and first cousin to cheddar, but softer, moister and less acidic." Crowley Cheese is truly an American original of the highest caliber.

Crowley Cheese is available in two-and-a-half- , five- , and twenty-five-pound waxed wheels at about $14.00, $26.00, and $110.00, respectively, depending on destination.

Conveniences: G, R, P, H **Credit Cards:** MC, V **Shipping:** U.S.—UPS; A&H—R; C—R

Gethsemani Farms

Highway 2479, Trappist, Kentucky 40051

502·549·3117

*T*his truly is cheese of a high order. The Cistercian monks of Gethsemani Farms (Abbey) in Trappist, Kentucky, have been making it by hand for decades and have gained a loyal following. It is a moist, full-bodied cheese made from an old-world process and from the best natural ingredients the monks can find.

Gethsemani Abbey is the oldest of sixteen Cistercian monasteries in the United States, having been established in 1848. The order itself goes back to 1098 A.D., when a group of Benedictine monks broke away from that order to establish their own more rigid order near the town of Citeaux, France, from which they take their name. The monks at Gethsemani still rise each day at three A.M., spending long hours at prayer and the making of their fine cheeses.

Gethsemani Farms offers three types of cheese: a young, mild variety, an aged, sharper type, and a smoked cheese. A variety of gift combinations are available. A whole three-pound wheel of any type sells for $14.75, shipping included. A beautiful handmade wood gift box with three-quarter wheels of mild, aged, and smoky cheeses (twelve ounces of each) is $14.25. Gethsemani Farms also makes excellent fruitcakes (see page 98).

Conveniences: G, R, P, H **Credit Cards:** none **Shipping:** U.S.—R, UPS; A&H—R; C—R

GETHSEMANI FARMS
Tomato Cheese Sauce

2 tablespoons butter
2 tablespoons flour
½ teaspoon minced fresh basil
1 cup tomato juice
1 cup water
¾ teaspoon salt
½ teaspoon black pepper
1 cup grated Trappist cheese

Melt butter; blend in flour and basil. Add tomato juice and water gradually, and cook, stirring constantly, until thick and smooth. Add salt, pepper, and cheese. Remove from heat and stir until cheese melts. Excellent on spaghetti. Makes six servings.

GETHSEMANI FARMS
Cheese-Rice Casserole

*P*repare thin white sauce: In 1-quart heavy saucepan melt 2 tablespoons butter; stir in 2 tablespoons flour and ½ teaspoon salt. Remove from heat; gradually stir in 2 cups milk. Cook over medium heat, stirring constantly, until thickened. Add 2 cups grated Trappist cheese, 1 tablespoon Worcestershire sauce, and a dash of red (cayenne) pepper. Combine with cooked rice, frozen peas, or corn. Put mixture in casserole dish, sprinkling with grated cheese. Bake in preheated 400°F oven for 10 minutes.

Goat Folks Farm

Tunison Road, Interlaken, New York 14847

607·532·4343

*I*an Zeiler, the cheese maker-owner of Goat Folks Farm, includes a sheet of rave reviews with his cheese. The *New York Times,* the *New York Daily News,* and *The New Yorker* magazine all liked the cheeses, as did the representatives of two of the most well-respected and renowned specialty markets in New York City. Dean & Deluca said: "It is simply an excellent cheese." Steven Jenkins of Fairway was moved to remark: "I love it!! I love it!!" But the best quotation of all is from Anita Zeiler, Ian's mother, who said: "It's the greatest cheese in the world."
Organically grown, herbicide- and insecticide-free feed keeps the goats happy on this small farm in the Finger Lakes region of New York. The mild, creamy, fresh chèvres produced here are unusual. Especially adapted for the American market, the cheeses are not as pungent as some chèvres.
The seven-to-eight-ounce containers are sold by the half-dozen ($4.00 each) or dozen ($3.50 each). The fresh chèvre freezes well, so order away and put the extra on ice. Add $6.00 an order east of the Mississippi for shipping and handling; $7.50 an order west of the Mississippi. Allow ten to fourteen days for delivery, unless the heat of summer necessitates a delay of a few more days. New Yorkers can find the cheeses at Bloomingdale's, Fairway, Zabar's, Dean & Deluca, Balducci's, and other markets.
Goat Folks offers some tasty serving suggestions, including using the cheese in a pasta primavera, in spaghetti carbonara, and with thinly sliced papaya wedges, sprinkled with raspberry vinegar and topped with toasted almonds.

Conveniences: D, R **Credit Cards:** MC, V **Shipping:** U.S.—X, UPS; A&H—X; C—X

Gethsemani Farms

Goat Folks Farm

The Goat Works, Inc.

R.D. 1, Box 57, Washington, New Jersey 07882

201·689·6899

"*G*oat Works was formed in January 1980 as the first producer of traditional chèvre in the United States," writes Gail LeCompte, the woman behind the scenes of this fifty-or-so goat farm. Her thirty-five acre plot in the Pohatcong Valley of New Jersey is home to Empress, Princess, Prince, Centurian, Abby, Joy, Smily, Giggles, and Ecstacy, a lineup of four-footed animals almost good enough to replace Santa's reindeer.
However lighthearted Gail LeCompte is about her goats, the cheese is a serious proposition, a commodity that can now be found at some of the best hotels and restaurants in New York and Washington. The aged Saanen, an unusual semi-hard slicing cheese, offers a mild, nutty flavor. At $7.50 a piece, it weighs in at about a pound. The four-ounce Mini Buche ($2.50 each) is a traditional chèvre, available plain, with garlic and herbs, or rolled in pepper.
The practicalities of shipping cheese allow Goat Works to serve only the contiguous United States and Canada. Shipping costs are ten percent of the order or $2.75, whichever is greater. And get those orders in early for Christmas; there's a strict December 1 deadline.

Conveniences: H, P **Credit Cards:** none **Shipping:** U.S.—UPS; C—UPS

The Goat Works, Inc.

Hawthorne Valley Farm

Hawthorne Valley Farm

RD 2 Box 225A, Ghent, New York 12075

518·672·7500

*T*he unique tastes of small-farm cheeses can not be discounted. Hawthorne Valley's raw-milk hard cheeses (officially, they're categorized as semisoft) have an almost nutty flavor that gives rise to comparisons with Emmentaler, Gruyère, and even cheddar.

A bio-dynamic farm run on Rudolph Steiner's ecological principles, Hawthorne Valley maintains itself as self-sufficiently as possible, using farm-produced manures and composts as only one of its "solutions." The cheese contains no additives, colorings, or preservatives, resulting in a soft yellow hue. The usual wax or cloth covering is missing; instead, an edible rind (the result of immersion in salt brine) acts to protect the cheese. The farm's emphasis on natural rhythms allows for seasonal—and interestingly subtle—variations in the cheese.

The bakery on the farm produces a rye sourdough and a wheat sourdough bread, which use homegrown, freshly milled grains when available. Following European traditions, no yeast, sweeteners, shortenings, oils, or preservatives are used—just flour, water, and salt.

The mild cheese sells for $3.50 a pound, while the medium, sharp, caraway, and smoked varieties sell for $4.00 a pound. Subtract a dollar a pound for orders of ten pounds or more. The breads are $1.70 for each one-and-three-quarter-pound loaf. Although gift packages are not in the farm's repertoire, they will enclose a gift note if requested.

Conveniences: P **Credit Cards:** MC, V **Shipping:** U.S.—UPS; A&H—UPS; C—UPS

Rawson Brook Farm

82

Little Rainbow Chèvre

Box 379, Rodman Road, Hillsdale, NY 12529
518·325·3351

*I*f you like bleu cheese, take pen in hand and write immediately for Barbara and Thomas Reed's "Berkshire Blue." Deposit your letter in the mail even if you're convinced you don't like goat cheese. This will change your mind. Available in half-pound wheels for $5.25, the cheese has an overwhelmingly delicious bleu taste that blends with the more delicate goat flavor.

Gourmet magazine picked out Little Rainbow Chèvre's Le Petit (Mûrir) Fromage: "Her Mûrir, a softly oozing morsel, is well worth asking for...." Full bodied and pungent, the Mûrir makes a fine match for crisp autumn apples; each package sells for $2.95 (for approximately four ounces).

Milder cheeses also have a home here. The soft, creamy Chèvre with Herbs offers Parsley, Sage, Rosemary, and Thyme; there is also Tarragon, Garlic, Basil, and Dill (which is good with a dab of butter on fresh green beans)—all for $2.25 each or four for $7.95, in four-and-a-half-ounce reusable containers.

Preservative- and chemical-free, Little Rainbow Chèvre's cheeses reflect the goodness the Reed family puts into them. Barbara, Tom, Robin, and Daniel are all involved in the business—whether it's the cheeses, the brown-and-white Toggenburg goats, or both.

Conveniences: G, R **Credit Cards:** none **Shipping:** U.S.—X, UPS; A&H—X; C—UPS

Rawson Brook Farm

Box 345, New Marlboro Road, Monterey, Massachusetts 02145
413·528·2138

*T*he delicate, unique chèvres that come from Rawson Brook Farm add a welcome taste to the growing roster of American-made cheeses. Developed from the French-trained expertise of Montrealer Martine Gadbois, Monterey chèvres come in four varieties: plain, with no salt added, with chives and garlic, and with wild thyme and olive oil.

The basic cheese is made with fresh goat's milk, an imported French lactic-acid starter culture, rennet, and salt. The chives and garlic are organically grown, and the thyme is picked from the neighboring meadows.

Visits to the farms are encouraged. The goats roam freely over the hillsides, and the does' diets consist of the pasture grasses and clover, as well as a daily ration of additive-free grains. A simple, forthright quality embraces both the cheese-making and the cheeses.

Shipping perishable items such as these cheeses does require care. The farm will ship to Massachusetts, Connecticut, Rhode Island, Vermont, New Hampshire, and the New York City area via UPS year-round. Orders going to the rest of New York, New Jersey, Washington, D.C., eastern Pennsylvania, northern Ohio, and Maine will be filled from September 15 to May 15 and shipped via UPS. Other destinations may receive the cheeses via UPS Second Day Air, but the extra postage will cost approximately $10.00 to $15.00.

The cheese freezes well, so you can buy in quantity (the minimum order is $20.00). A half-case (twelve four-ounce cups) runs for $20.00; a full case (twenty-four four-ounce cups), $36.00. A case of one-pound tubs (six in all) comes to $33.00. Feel free to mix the varieties. Add $4.00 to the order for the cost of the reusable insulated foam boxes with refreezable ice packets.

For Christmas gifts, there's a package that includes four of the cups; a 4.2-ounce, stronger pepper-coated cheese; and a copy of *Chèvre! The Goat Cheese Cookbook* by Laura Chenel and Linda Siegfried. Wrapped and shipped, it costs $25.00.

Conveniences: G, R **Credit Cards:** none **Shipping:** U.S.—UPS

Shelburne Farms

Shelburne, Vermont 05482

802·985·8686

*W*hen referring to Shelburne Farms, it's hard to know which to talk about first: the absolutely superb farmhouse cheddar or the magnificent grounds of the farms (see box). The beautifully packaged cheese comes close to perfection in taste and texture. Choose from a sampler of six half-pound bars ($19.00), three one-pound bars ($18.00), or the two- and four-pound blocks. The medium blocks are $12.00 and $23.00 for two and four pounds, respectively; sharp blocks, $13.00 and $24.00; and extra sharp, $14.00 and $25.00.

Shelburne Farms also offers very well-put-together gift assortments with top-quality Vermont products: Champlain Chocolates (see page 46), Shelburne Orchards apples, Chuck and Carla Conway's European Country Bread (made on the farm), and David Marvin's Grade A Maple Syrup. (You may even ask for Dark Amber Syrup instead of the more recognizable Medium Amber.) A simple box includes a 3.9-ounce box of chocolates, one pound of cheese, and a pint of syrup for $19.00. The Deluxe Gift Box is a treasure trove, with two pounds of cheddar, one-half pint of syrup, one-half pound of Shelburne Farms honey, one pound of sourdough French bread, a ten-ounce jar of Strawberry Amaretto Conserve, and a 3.9-ounce box of chocolates. Holiday orders should be in by December 10. Write for their catalog for more information on the assortments and on the farm itself.

Conveniences: D, G, H, P **Credit Cards:** AE, MC, V **Shipping:** U.S.—UPS; A&H—R, X, UPS; C—R

Shelburne Farms

RAWSON BROOK FARM
Chèvre Serving Suggestions

- Monterey Chèvre can be served from the cup as a dip or a spread. For more elegant table use, unmold the cheese onto a plate.

- Chèvre can be sprinkled with pepper or fresh herbs, marinated in olive oil and served with french bread.

- Monterey Chèvre can be formed into ½-inch-thick patties, dipped in olive oil, then in cracker crumbs and baked for 45 minutes in a 350°F preheated oven.

- You can make sauces for vegetables and meats by adding a container of Monterey Chèvre to the cooking juices.

- The chèvre with chives and garlic is a tasty addition to omelettes and makes a good sandwich spread when mixed with avocado.

- For a wonderful dessert, mix honey or sugar with the chèvre and top it with fresh fruit.

Shelburne Farms

*J*ust off Route 7, six miles south of Burlington, Vermont, stands a turreted house of stone that rises above beautiful landscaped grounds. The majestic house and its surrounding buildings, all designed by Robert Henderson Robertson, make up Shelburne Farms, a 1,000-acre agricultural estate that is entered on the National Register of Historic Places.

Dr. William Seward and Lila Vanderbilt Webb acquired the property, which included thirty small farms, in 1885, with the vision to set up a model farm and a self-sufficient country estate. Situated on the shores of Lake Champlain in Shelburne, Vermont, Shelburne Farms remains as proof to their success. Aesthetically, philosophically, and practically, the Farms offer something to please even the most severe pundit.

Today, Shelburne Farms is undergoing restoration. The farmhouse operations and the products make this a special stop along any traveler's New England ramblings, and if that's not enough, the grounds themselves are worthy of the trip. Frederick Law Olmstead, the man who designed New York City's Central Park, lent his skills to the pastures, rolling hills, and wooded areas, helped by Gifford Pinchot, a founder of the American Conservation and Forestry Movement. Together, they relocated roads, planted forests, and recontoured fields.

Visitors are welcome: The Cheese Shop is open all year, every day, from 9 A.M. to 5 P.M., but the tour—which includes a cheese-tasting and stops at the formal gardens, the great barns, and a dairy barn—runs at 10 A.M. and 2 P.M. every day only from June to October 15. You'll also get a peek at the largest registered herd of Brown Swiss in New England, fed entirely from grass and legume hay grown organically on the farm. The property, a nonprofit agricultural land trust, supports itself largely through membership contributions, grants, and educational program fees, in addition to Cheese Shop sales.

JOHN WILLIAM LUND

CHAPTER ELEVEN

Fish and Caviar

California Sunshine Fine Foods Inc.

144 King Street, San Francisco, California 94107

415·543·3007

*R*ussian and Iranian caviar may still be the most sought-after luxury food in the world—it is certainly the most expensive—but American caviar is gaining ground fast, due in large part to the efforts of Swedish-born San Franciscans Mats and Defne Engstrom, owners of California Sunshine Inc.

Since 1970, the Engstroms have been busy reviving the American caviar industry, which flourished in the early part of this century, but which was fished out and became extinct for roughly sixty years. Now, American caviar outsells Russian caviar in America six to one, and many experts believe it's just as good as the Russian type, especially considering that American caviar is up to seventy-five percent cheaper.

Tsar Nicoulai Spoonbill Sturgeon Caviar, a supreme small black roe, is available from California Sunshine in a seven-ounce tin for $30.00. Then there is the excellent, crisp Tsar Nicoulai American Gold Pearl Caviar, a larger egg with a distinctive flavor, at $20.00 for a 6.5-ounce tin. Tsar Nicoulai American Golden Caviar, another excellent gold caviar with its own fine attributes, sells for $20.00 per 6.4-ounce tin.

Conveniences: P, D **Credit Cards:** MC, V **Shipping:** U.S.—X, UPS

Ekone Oyster Company

Star Route, Box 465, South Bend, Washington 98586

206·875·5494

*E*kone, the Chinook Indian name for "good spirit," lends the proper tone of respect for nature that Nick and Joanne Jambor seem to have for their smoked oysters. These delicacies are full, plump specimens—not pieces or seconds. The critters come from Willapa Bay, one of the cleanest in the United States.

Oyster-farming à la Ekone begins with a method of stringing the oyster "seeds" above the ocean floor, a method that allows the mollusks to "feed better, feel better, and grow fatter than their relations on the ground." The alderwood smoke just adds to their tastiness.

The handpicked smoked oysters are vacuum-packed without oil, a detail many diet-conscious gourmets may want to note. The minimum order of one pound goes for $22.00; add $15.00 for each additional pound. The shipping, included in the price for the contiguous U.S. and Alaska, is slightly higher for Hawaii. The Jambors request that you get your Christmas orders in early, as there are no shipments after December 16.

Conveniences: H, P **Credit Cards:** none **Shipping:** U.S.—UPS; A&H—UPS

Ekone Oyster Company

Jake's Famous Products

401 Southwest 12th Street, Portland, Oregon 97205

503·226·1420

*I*f you've ever traveled in the Pacific Northwest, you may well be familiar with Jake's restaurants; the original, in Portland, dates from 1892. The Famous Products line was created to offer the restaurant's turn-of-the-century traditions to discerning customers for home use. Jake's World Famous Canned Clam Chowder recipe took six months to develop, with a result that *Bon Appetit* magazine proclaimed "the best damn chowder in the country." A white New England chowder—you have to add milk, and a dab of butter is good—Jake's measures up to some of the best, thick homemades.

The company also provides an unusually good Tartar Sauce with Dill (it comes plain, too) and a Cocktail Sauce that may tempt you to use it as a dip for crunchy crudités.

The products can be found at Macy's, Meier & Frank, and Neiman-Marcus if you're shopping in person. If you choose to purchase them by mail, try Norm Thompson, Hickory Farms, Figi's, REI, and Eddie Bauer. If you'd rather buy in bulk you can write directly to the company for more information. Holiday requests should be in a month early.

JAKE'S FAMOUS PRODUCTS
Sesame Scallops

1½ cups cornstarch
1½ cups flour
1 tablespoon garlic base
2½ cups beer
1 teaspoon salt
1 teaspoon white pepper
1 pound sea scallops
1 cup sesame seeds
1 cup soy sauce
2 cups water
½ cup sherry
1 teaspoon finely chopped fresh garlic
1 cup sugar
1 teaspoon freshly grated ginger
6 green onions, chopped

In a mixing bowl, combine cornstarch, flour, and garlic base (bottled minced garlic available in the vegetable department of major supermarkets). With a whip, slowly mix while adding beer until you reach a smooth pancake-batter consistency, then mix in salt and pepper, and set aside.

Slice scallops into medallions and place 4-ounces each on a skewer. Put in tempura batter, roll in sesame seeds and deep-fry at 350°F for 7 minutes. Combine remaining ingredients to make sashimi sauce. Serve on the side.

Makes four servings.

JAKE'S FAMOUS PRODUCTS
Baked Salmon Steaks

3 pounds salmon steaks, cut 1 inch thick
¼ pound mushrooms, minced
1 medium onion, minced
2 tablespoons minced parsley
¼ cup butter or margarine
½ cup dry sherry
⅓ cup fine bread or corn flake crumbs

Lay the steaks in a well-greased shallow casserole. Mix the mushrooms, onion, and parsley and spread over the fish. Cut the butter into bits and dot over the top. Pour the sherry and bake in a preheated moderate oven, 350°F, for 15 minutes.

Spread the steaks with the crumbs and continue baking another 10 or 15 minutes, or until fish flakes readily. Baste 2 or 3 times during baking. Serves six.

Jake's Famous Products

Latta's

P.O. Box 1377, Newport, Oregon 97365

503·265·7675

*T*he labels on Latta's smoked Pacific seafoods are so aesthetically arresting, you almost wonder if what's inside can live up to the show. But as you'll discover, that's no problem. Latta's premium smoked fish, oysters, and shrimp are absolute tops in taste, too. They arrive ready to turn out onto a plate with crackers, and thus make a simple yet exquisite cocktail snack. Or use them with one of Latta's recipes for a more sophisticated hor d'oeuvre or entree.

Latta's canned fresh-smoked seafoods include Smoked Salmon, Smoked Albacore, Smoked Oysters, Smoked Pacific Shrimp, Smoked Albacore Tuna, Smoked Sturgeon, and Smoked Chinook Salmon. They come in six-ounce tins and sell for $6.95 each, except for the sturgeon, which is $7.95. Latta's Captain's Choice is a gift box of six of the above tins for $38.95, plus shipping. It is beautifully packaged with real seashells and a seafood cookbook.

Latta's has a variety of at least a hundred other worthy specialty products, from their Indian Fry Bread Mix to their Rhubarb-Apple Chutney. Send for their catalog and pick your favorites.

Conveniences: G, P, R, H **Credit Cards:** AE, MC, V **Shipping:** U.S.—UPS; A&H—UPS

Merchant Adventurers Tea & Spice Co.

70 Hollins Drive, Santa Cruz, California 95060

408·356·8191

*C*anadian Golden Caviar is the finest roe of the Canadian Lake Whitefish, harvested just before freeze-over from the cool, clear, clean lakes of northern Canada. This particular brand of small-egg Malossol caviar is pasteurized and salted only very lightly so as to retain the original crisp texture and subtle flavor.
Canadian Golden Caviar has won two distinguished Gold Medals for flavor and show quality at the 1980 and 1984 World Culinary Olympics in Frankfurt, West Germany. Also, it has been served at embassy receptions in London, Brussels, Paris, Tokyo, and New York.
Canadian Golden Caviar comes in sets of three 1.75-ounce jars that sell for $10.00 per set. Recipes are included.

Conveniences: R, P, D **Credit Cards:** MC, V **Shipping:** U.S.—X, UPS; A&H—R; C—R

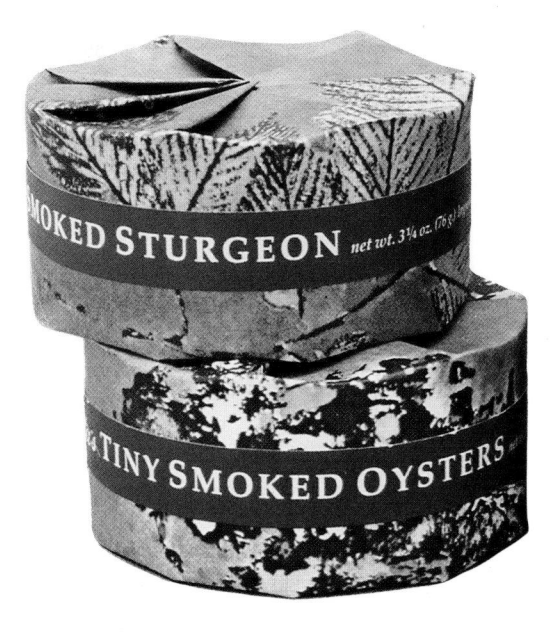

Latta's

MERCHANT ADVENTURERS TEA & SPICE CO.
The Classic Caviar Service

TOAST FOR CAVIAR:

You can use either: 1 baguette of french bread, sliced. Brush each side with butter and bake 5–8 minutes. The Russian method uses black pumpernickel bread, thinly sliced. Americans sometimes use rye biscuits, Wasa bread, melba toast rounds, or any other very hard biscuit.

Side Dishes:
   Arrange the following attractively, each in its own separate small dish.
Dish 1. 1 cup sour cream
Dish 2. Finely chopped whites of 2 hard-boiled eggs
Dish 3. Finely chopped yolks of 2 hard-boiled eggs
Dish 4. ¾ cup finely chopped chives
Dish 5. 2 lemons cut in small wedges, for squeezing on the canapé
Dish 6. Lots of Canadian Golden Caviar...at least 2 jars to start.
Keep rest, unopened, in the refrigerator.
   Let the guests help themselves, spreading any combination of caviar and side dishes to suit their taste. The fun is in experimenting with different combinations of caviar, chives, sour cream, and eggs...each with a squeeze of lemon for flavor.

MERCHANT ADVENTURERS TEA & SPICE CO.
Russian Mousse

1 English cucumber, peeled
12 hard-boiled eggs
1 teaspoon salt
6 green onions, chopped
⅓ cup warm water
2 tablespoons lemon juice
1 package unflavored gelatin
¾ cup mayonnaise
1 cup sour cream
1 teaspoon Dijon mustard
Salt and pepper, to taste
2 (1.75 ounces) jars Canadian Golden Caviar

Cut half of the cucumber into small pieces and slice the other half evenly to use for garnish. Mash the eggs, reserve ⅓ cup for garnish. Combine salt and ⅔ of the chopped onions with the eggs and add to the chopped up cucumber. Reserve the other ⅓ of the onions for garnish.
   Put water and lemon juice into a heavy saucepan. Sprinkle with gelatin. Allow it to soften for 5 minutes. Heat at a low temperature. Put mayonnaise into a bowl. Add ½ the sour cream and the 1 teaspoon mustard. Add gelatin mix and blend. Combine with egg and cucumber mixture. Salt and pepper to taste. Put into a greased Springform pan or a quiche dish. Refrigerate for 2 hours.
   Unmold mousse onto serving platter lined with lettuce leaves or parsley. Spread top with remaining ½ cup sour cream. Arrange caviar in the center. Ring with a border of chopped eggs, green onion, and cucumber slices. Serve with pumpernickel bread.

Poriloff American Caviars

PUREPAK FOODS, INC.
47-39 49th St., Woodside, New York 11377

718·784·3344

*F*or caviar lovers who are also patriots, Poriloff offers a scintillating selection of America's finest caviar. First, in price and rarity, is their Pasteurized American Sturgeon Caviar, a fine black caviar culled from the sturgeon of various rivers and lakes in the southeastern United States, with a flavor that stands up excellently to the best Caspian Sea caviar. It sells at $8.60 for one ounce, $16.30 for two ounces, and $31.00 for four ounces.
Slightly less rare, though no less distinct or delicious, is Poriloff's pasteurized Salmon Caviar from Oregon, Washington, and Alaska. These eggs are larger than those of the sturgeon and have a beautiful red-orange color. A two-ounce jar is $4.95, four ounces is $9.25.
Poriloff also has a Golden Whitefish Caviar, which comes from the Great Lakes. These are small crisp eggs with a sparkling golden color and subtle flavor all their own. They are priced at $3.50 for two ounces, $5.50 for four ounces. Order directly from Poriloff or find these caviars in hundreds of gourmet shops throughout the country.

Conveniences: P, D **Credit Cards:** AE **Shipping:** U.S.—UPS

BRIAN LEATART

CHAPTER TWELVE

Coffees, Teas
and Other Beverages

Alpenglow Sparkling Cider

LINDEN BEVERAGE COMPANY, INC.
Route 1, Box 35, Linden, Virginia 22642
703·635·5481

*A*lpenglow sparkling cider is a great source of vitamin C with only eighty-five calories in six ounces, but its real appeal comes from the blended Virginia-grown winesap and red delicious apples, a marriage of sweetness and body. Alcohol-free, the cider won't turn; its yeast particles are killed during pasteurization, so its shelf life stretches to at least eighteen months. But we doubt it would last that long before someone "uncorked" the bottle. This no-sugar, no-preservatives beverage also serves as the base for a number of fanciful drinks: Freezeland Float, Stonewall Jackson, and Bruised Apple Punch to name a few.

The sparkling cider and mulled sparkling cider are available in 6.3-ounce (187 milliliter) bottles, twenty-four to a case. Minimum order is one case at $13.85, plus shipping, which will be via UPS. If you can't get enough, you can place a six-case (twelve to a case) minimum order of the 25.4-ounce (750 milliliters) bottles at $15.60, plus shipping, a case. These will be delivered by common carrier. Neiman-Marcus, Hecht's, Woodward and Lothrop, Leggett's, and Thalheimer's also carry this prized cider.

Conveniences: D, P, R **Credit Cards:** none **Shipping:** U.S.—common carrier, UPS

ALPENGLOW
Sparkling Cider

Freezeland Float Allow one pint of vanilla ice cream to soften. Stir in one bottle of Alpenglow and a dash of cinnamon. Blend well. Pour into a tall glass and top with a scoop of ice cream. Sprinkle with cinnamon. Makes four to six servings.

Lee's Traveler Fill a 6-ounce glass with 1½ ounces Bowman's Virginia Vodka. Add crushed ice and fill with Alpenglow. Garnish with a slice of apple.

Hot Pippin In a saucepan, bring 2 bottles of Alpenglow to just-boiling. Remove from heat. Add 2½ cups dark rum. Ladle into mugs. Add a teaspoon butter, a cinnamon stick, and a whole clove to each. Serve at once. Makes ten servings.

Red Delicious Punch Pour 2 bottles of Alpenglow into a punch bowl. Mix in one quart cranberry juice. Float a frozen ice ring and garnish with sprigs of mint.

Gillies Coffee Company

Gillies Coffee Company

160 Bleecker Street, New York, New York 10012

212·260·2130

Gillies is America's oldest coffee merchant, having been established in 1840 by Wright Gillies. From the beginning, Gillies' primary goal was to find the best available coffee of each variety and offer it to his customers at reasonable prices. Seven generations have passed, and the company's objectives remain the same. While the coffee market in America has developed into a massive business where quality is talked about but seldom delivered, Gillies has changed only in that it has refined the processing of the world's great coffee beans into an involved science, in the sole interest of bringing you better coffee.

Gillies' coffee categories include unblended coffees such as Hawaii Kona, Sumatra Mandheeling, Jamaica High Mountain Peaberry; blended coffees such as Mr. Gillies' original breakfast blend called Perfection, a strong yet mellow blend known as Norwegian Wood, and others; dark roast coffees like Vienna Roast, Turkish Roast, Italian Roast, and French Roast; decaffeinated coffees in at least three varieties that all go through a completely natural water-decaffeination process; flavored coffees, which are selected coffees with certain spices added; and decaffeinated flavored coffees. In other words, Gillies has all the best coffees in all the combinations and variations. The prices are reasonable, many as low as $4.25 a pound, and Gillies' gold packaging is exquisite. Gillies also knows and sells the world's finest teas.

Conveniences: H, D, P, G **Credit Cards:** MC, V, ($15.00) **Shippping:** U.S.—UPS

Grace Tea Company Limited

Grace Tea Company Limited

50 West 17th Street, New York, New York 10011

212·255·2935

Producing a fine tea is a complex process that depends on such factors as the type of tea bush, its growing areas, elevation of the estate (plantation), weather, time of harvest, selection and method of picking leaves, withering (moisture reduction), fermentation, firing, and grading. Since 1962, Grace Tea Company has carefully attended to these factors, with the result of a consistent line of excellent-quality teas.

You neeedn't be a tea connoisseur to appreciate the subtle differences between the teas offered by Grace Tea. The company has developed a relatively simple selection of blends that anyone can readily learn to distinguish and enjoy. They offer five black teas, including Superb Darjeeling 6000, Winey Keemun English Breakfast, Lapsang Souchong Smoky No. 1, Earl Grey Superior Mixture, and their own Connoisseur Special Blend, as well as a Formosa Oolong Supreme and a blend they call Before the Rain Jasmine. All of the teas come in a handsome metal canister and are priced at $9.15 for eight ounces, except for the Darjeeling, which is $10.15, and the Formosa Oolong, which is $12.15. A Sampler Tray of five two-ounce canisters is $21.50. Add $2.75 for all orders up to $30.00.

Conveniences: G, P **Credit Cards:** none **Shipping:** U.S.—UPS; A&H—R; C—R

Harney & Sons Limited Fine Teas

Salisbury, Connecticut 06068
203·435·9218

Harney & Sons specializes in the premium teas of Ceylon and India but carries a wide variety of the world's teas, including Formosa Oolong, Jasmine, Keemun, Earl Grey, and Darjeeling. All teas are bought in small, controlled lots to assure freshness, and the Harneys do all their own blending so as to maintain constant flavor quality. Also, Harney & Sons packs 175 tea bags to the pound (forty grains) rather than two hundred bags to the pound, as do many other companies, thus giving each tea bag more flavor.

All Harney & Sons Teas are priced at $6.75 for an eight-ounce box, except for Darjeeling, which sells for $7.25 for eight ounces. Three-box gift assortments are also available.

Conveniences: G, P **Credit Cards:** none **Shipping:** U.S.—UPS; A&H—UPS; C—UPS

Harney & Sons Limited Fine Teas

Rainbow Tea & Spicery

P.O. Box 293, Clackamas, Oregon 97015-0293

503·657·3055

*Y*ou've heard of spiced teas, herbal teas, and flavored coffees. So had Patricia McCormick, but while she liked these popular drinks, she always loved hot cocoa better. When she started her business in 1979, she began by marketing her own spiced and herbal tea concoctions, leaving the old favorite—traditional cocoa—out of the picture. Then, a while later, she got the idea of adding spices to cocoa. The idea was new, the taste was phenomenal, and it had no caffeine. Spicey Cocoa, as Patty subsequently named it, has since become her most popular product. Customers keep pouring in, and Ms. McCormick continues to invent delightful new flavors.

Now, Rainbow Tea and Spicery offers six different Spicey Cocoas—an Original Blend with a delightfully spicy accent, Spicey Cherry Cocoa, Spicey Mint Cocoa, Spicey Amaretto Cocoa, Spicey Orange Cocoa, and Spicey Kahlua Cocoa. They come with excellent recipes, such as one for Mandarin Orange Truffle Sauce. The cocoas come in handsome six-ounce tins for $5.95, plus shipping.

Conveniences: R, P, H **Credit Cards:** MC, V, ($10.00) **Shipping:** U.S.—UPS; A&H—R; C—R

Rainbow Tea & Spicery

Starbucks Coffee and Tea

4555 University Way Northeast, Seattle, Washington 98105

206·447·1575

*S*tarbucks is famous for quality coffee and tea in the Pacific Northwest. They roast thirty varieties of only the finest 100 percent *arabica* coffees daily in Seattle and market them through their own retail stores, fine restaurants, and to a growing number of mail-order customers throughout North America. If you have a favorite, hard-to-find type of coffee, chances are you can get it from Starbucks. Or try one of their house specialties, such as their Yukon blend—a dark, rich, nutty coffee with remarkable flavor. The average price per pound of Starbucks coffee ranges from $4.50 to $7.00.

Starbucks teas are selectively imported from China, India, Sri Lanka, and Taiwan, and are carefully blended by Starbucks' expert tasters. The teas are quite reasonably priced, and come in one-half-pound packages.

Starbucks also has a full line of quality coffee makers, coffee grinders, and coffee-related hardware that is available by mail order.

Conveniences: R, P, H **Credit Cards:** MC, V **Shipping:** U.S.—R, X, UPS; A&H—R, X, UPS; C—R, X, UPS

Sunrise Teas & Spices Inc.

P.O. Box 11214, Reno, Nevada 89510

702·322·4031

*B*eautifully gift-packed herbal teas are the specialty of this Reno, Nevada, company. Spiced Peach, Fruited Rum, Jasmine Almond, and Spiced Raspberry are a few of their more exotic herbals, but they also carry better known ones like Cinnamon-Apple, Orange Spice, and Peppermint Spice, as well as a couple of proper teas including Earl Grey and English Breakfast. A Twelve-Pack Tea Sampler includes twelve types of tea, six tea bags of each, with each type individually boxed. It sells for $12.00. A Four-Pack Tea Sampler includes four different teas for $5.00. Sunrise Teas & Spices has a variety of tea gift combinations. Typically, they include a sampling of the teas, packed in an attractive and reusable wicker basket with two ceramic mugs. Depending on the size, they range in price from $12.00 to $25.00. They make great warming gifts for fall and winter.

Conveniences: G, P, R, D **Credit Cards:** MC, V **Shipping:** U.S.—UPS; A&H—UPS; C—R, UPS

Sunrise Teas & Spices Inc.

CHAPTER THIRTEEN

Fruitcakes

BMG Enterprises, Inc.

230 West Huron, Suite 6W, Chicago, Illinois 60610

312·787·2630

*T*he exquisite nutty flavor of this moist, raisin-filled loaf would be special enough by itself, but pair it with a sweet, salubrious dose of premium Irish whiskey, as Butch McGuire does, and the palate virtually palpitates with pleasure. McGuire and his wife, Mary, have been making their loaf now for upward of thirty years, serving it from their Chicago restaurant, McGuire's. As the rich loaf's fame grew, the McGuires were all but forced to offer it to a wider audience. McGuire's Irish Whiskey Loaf is supreme with afternoon tea, or with a dollop of cream after dinner. Each one-pound loaf is soaked with three full ounces of whiskey and costs $9.95. A two-pound loaf sells for $17.50.

Conveniences: P, D **Credit Cards:** AE, MC, V **Shipping:** U.S.—UPS; A&H—UPS; C—UPS

Eilenberger's Bakery

512 North John Street, Palestine, Texas 75801

214·729·2253

*D*reams of the land of opportunity prompted F.H. Eilenberger's parents to leave their home in Leipzig, Germany, in 1881 and come to America. In 1898, young F.H. moved to Palestine, Texas, and at the age of twenty-one opened his own bakery. Eilenberger spent fifty years building a reputation for great old-world baked goods, and finally sold the business to his sons and son-in-law in 1948. With the founder's strong reputation and recipes behind them, the new proprietors forged ahead and broke into the world market of fruitcakes, concentrating their efforts on Eilenberger's secret recipes for Pecan Cake, Australian Apricot Cake, and original Fruit Cake. Eilenberger's has since won two International Gold Medal Awards at the famous world food show in Vienna, Austria, and Eilenberger's Bakery in Palestine is now a Texas State Historical Landmark.
All Eilenberger fruitcakes come in two-pound, three-pound, and five-pound sizes.

Conveniences: H, R, P, G **Credit Cards:** AE, MC, V **Shipping:** U.S.—R, X, UPS; A&H—R; C—R

Gethsemani Farms

Highway 247, Trappist, Kentucky 40051

502·549·3117

*I*n addition to their fine line of handmade cheeses (see page 80), the Cistercian monks at Gethsemani Abbey produce one of the best fruitcakes in the southern United States. It too is handmade daily by the monks themselves, who don't stop short of adding to their old-world recipe perhaps the richest specialty of the region—aged Kentucky bourbon. The result is well-nigh heavenly.
Gethsemani's Trappist Fruit Cake is a well-raised cake, thickly studded with highest-quality nuts and fruits and baked to a lovely dark brown color. It comes in two-and-a-half- and five-pound rings, which are packaged in handsome red tins with the Gethsemani Farms logo, at $13.00 and $23.00, respectively, postage included.

Conveniences: G, R, P, H **Credit Cards:** none **Shipping:** U.S.—R, UPS; A&H—R; C—R

Eilenberger's Bakery

Gethsemani Farms

Matthews 1812 House Inc.

Metz Baking Company

201 South 5th, P.O. Box 457, Beatrice, Nebraska 68310

402·223·2358 or 1·800·228·4030

*I*t need not be the holiday season for this delicious fruitcake to elevate your spirits. In addition to high quantities of premium-quality seedling pecans, English walnuts, nonpareil almonds, imported pineapple, and fancy golden raisins, Grandma's Master Fruit Cake is rich with the best 84-proof brandy, 86-proof rum, and 100-proof bonded bourbon. The recipe for this special cake made its way from Germany to Beatrice, Nebraska, more than seventy years ago. It stayed hidden for a few years, until 1917, when two bakers discovered and tested it. They decided that making the cake, which stores well, would be a good way to stay busy during the slack summer months. They baked the fruitcakes in the summer and sold them in the winter. People loved them, and Metz Baking Company hasn't stopped making them since. Grandma's Master Fruit Cake is available in a two-pound loaf, which comes in a beautiful gold-embossed gift box, for about $12.00, or in three- or five-pound rings, which come in collectible tins illustrated with authentic pioneer quilt designs, at about $17.00 and $26.00. They are also sold at Bullock's, Woolf Brothers, Macy's, and Gimbels.

Conveniences: G, P, H, D **Credit Cards:** MC, V **Shipping:** U.S.—UPS; A&H—UPS; C—UPS

Matthews 1812 House Inc.

15 Whitcomb Hill Road, Cornwall Bridge, Connecticut 06754
203·672·0149

*D*eanna Matthews' customers are her best publicity. In 1984, one fruitcake aficionado sent a cellophane-wrapped and ribboned gift to each of the seventy-eight members of the United States Air Force Band. Needless to say, Deanna's Heirloom Fruit & Nut Cakes are among the very best. The fresh egg, butter, and cream batter holds together the crisp pecans and plump, dried apricots, dates, and raisins. No peels, rinds, candied fruits, or preservatives are added to these sweet yet tart cakes. For apricot lovers, there's an even tarter version: the Heritage Brandied Apricot Cake that's out of this world. The cakes come in one-and-a-half-pound ($13.25) boxes or three-pound round tins.
Another delight is the buttery, moist Lemon Rum Sunshine Cake, a beautifully molded tube-cake that puts a plain pound cake to shame. The one-and-three-quarter-pound confection costs $15.50 and comes in a round gift tin.
Matthews offers other tastefully packaged treats that make wonderful presents, and you can send your own gift cards to be placed in the package. Other possible presents are Spice Ships (after-dinner pastilles), a honey mustard sauce, Cumberland sauce, homemade jams and jellies, minted chocolates, chocolate-dipped apricots, and nut selections. The 1812 House catalog also describes gift assortments, including three-month and six-month gift plans. Some of the items are seasonal (the fruitcakes are available year-round), so write for more details.

Conveniences: G, P **Credit Cards:** AE, MC, V **Shipping:** U.S.—R, X, UPS; A&H—R, X; C—R, X

Miss King's Kitchens Inc.

5302 Highway 75 North, Sherman, Texas 75090
214·893·8151

*T*he sumptuous selection of treats that issues from the ovens of Miss King's Kitchens is unique, delicious, and most deserving of high honors. First, consider the Super Macadamia Hawaiian Fruitcake—a masterpiece of baking, thick with pineapple chunks, choice coconut, and mounds of macadamias. This rare delight is impossible to confuse with other fruitcakes. But if you are a fruitcake fanatic, Miss King's has other interesting options, including Butter Rum, Pecan Royale, and Grand Marnier Fruitcakes, all available in a variety of sizes up to two pounds, which range from $9.00 to $21.00. The two-pound Macadamia Fruitcake comes in a beautiful reusable round tin for $21.00.
Miss King's also features an assortment of traditional Southern Tea Cakes, which are airy flavored cakes textured very like a fine pound cake and eminently suitable for afternoon tea. They contain no preservatives, yet they retain their moisture and subtle flavor characters remarkably well. Flavors include English Cream, Strawberry, Lemon Cream, and Chocolate. Various combinations and sizes are available for $8.00 to $16.00.
Chocolate chip cookies aren't anything new, but try to find some as healthful as Miss King's. Hers are delicious *and* all-natural. She uses whole-wheat flour, raw sugar, and honey, not to mention gobs of pure chocolate chips and fine pecans. They come in a beautiful seventeen-and-three-quarter-ounce tin for about $10.00.

Conveniences: G, P, H, D **Credit Cards:** none **Shipping:** U.S.—R, X, UPS; C—UPS or customer's request

Miss King's Kitchens Inc.

The Society Bakery

The Society Bakery

Box 877, 104 Charles Street, Boston, Massachusetts 02114

617·648·4695

*T*his fancy bakery on Boston's Beacon Hill has achieved nationwide fame on the sole basis of its delicious premium-quality aged fruitcake—called the Classic Fruitcake. Each one of these handmade, hand-decorated fruitcakes contains 25 percent pecans, as well as apricots, raisins, cherries, and figs, and is aged at least one month. It is the aging, say the cake's inventors, that is responsible for the rich, moist, mellow flavor that makes the Classic classic. Just before leaving the Society Bakery, each Classic Fruitcake is wrapped in parchment and packed in a distinctive red box with a custom gold label. The one-and-a-half-pound loaf sells for $12.00, plus $2.00 shipping.

For those who love rich cake but are less fond of fruitcake, the Society Bakery offers a superb Sun-Dried Apricot Cake, a tart rich cake that contains 27 percent dried apricots by weight, pecans, dates, raisins, and rum, but no candied fruit. A one-and-a-half-pound cake costs $12.00, plus $2.00 shipping.

The Society Bakery has a variety of selected assortment samplers that contain other specialties, along with their wonderful fruitcakes.

Conveniences: G, P, H **Credit Cards:** MC, V **Shipping:** U.S.—UPS

CHAPTER FOURTEEN

Breads, Breadstuffs, Pasta and Rice

<u>*Bon Mélange, Inc.*</u>

115 Davis Avenue, Pass Christian, Mississippi 39571
601·452·3258

*T*here's nothing like the smell of fresh bread baking. Unfortunately, home-baked bread is becoming as rare as neighborhood soda fountains and wooden pinball machines. Bon Mélange's mixes for Lazy River Herb and Lazy River Dill breads entice you into the kitchen once again. A can of stale beer transforms the herbs into two loaves of appealingly aromatic bread. Both packets ring in under $5.00, plus $2.50 an order for shipping.
Try supplementing your order with Ev's Poppy Almond Cake Mix ($6.95), which comes complete with vial of almond extract, or Malee Hearin's Mississippi Mud Mix, a very chocolate cake with pecans and chocolate sauce running through it ($6.95).
Bon Mélange also offers charming gift packs: Supper For Eight with soup, bread, and Ev's Poppy Cake or Mississippi Mud Mix packed in a napkin-lined breadbasket, or Sunday Supper, a small basket with soup mix and one package for herb or dill bread. (See page 111 for catalog information.)

Bon Mélange, Inc.   Culinary Products Group

Culinary Products Group

GOLDRUSH ENTERPRISES
122 East Grand Avenue, South San Francisco, California 94080
415·871·0340
1·800·531·2039

*S*ourdough, the ore of Goldrush Enterprises, dates back five thousand years as a leavening agent. During the Gold Rush era this "wild yeast" was "considered as valuable as gold itself" by many families who used it to leaven their flour products. San Francisco and sourdough are inextricably entwined; the city's sourdough bread heads up a list of culinary treasures of the Golden Gate area. You don't have to visit to indulge in the tangy-flavored goodness of the fresh loaves. Goldrush's Old-Fashioned San Francisco Sourdough Starter Packet (one-half ounce for $2.25) includes starter that originates from the company's mother culture, which has been alive and active for over one hundred years. Recipes, also included, explain how to begin the process as well as how to use the starter for browned loaves of French bread, waffles, or pancakes. The procedure does take time—the results are worth it—so Goldrush also offers instant mixes for biscuits, pancakes, and waffles. A variation on a sourdough theme: The company also came up with easy mixes for oatmeal muffins and cookies, bran muffins and cornbread—all with a slight and deliciously saucy zest. They sell for $2.50 to $4.00. Watch for Goldrush Products at Macy's and Neiman-Marcus, too.

Conveniences: D, P, R **Credit Cards:** MC, V, ($5.00) **Shipping:** U.S.—UPS; A&H—R; C—R

DiCamillo Bakery

811 Linwood Avenue, Niagara Falls, New York 14305

716·282·2341

*I*f you love fine bread and/or cookies—and who doesn't?—you're in for a great treat with the premium goodies of this family-owned-and-operated Niagara Falls bakery. Working with the classic recipes that grandfather DiCamillo brought with him to America when he immigrated from Italy's Abbruzzi region in the 1920s, the current DiCamillo clan has mastered a class of rich, dry breads and biscuits that will take your tastebuds places they've never been before.

First and foremost in their biscuit collection is the now-famous Biscotti di Vino, a dry, faintly sweet biscuit made with California red wine and rolled in sesame seeds. It's perfect for cocktail parties, with wine or espresso, or simply as a sophisticated snack. Other DiCamillo variations on this theme include Biscotti allo Champagne, an extremely lush biscuit made with white wine champagne, port, sherry, and hazelnuts. For taste and simple elegance, they are unparalleled. If you're serving pâté or caviar, do it justice with DiCamillo's Biscotti Angelica, which are thin slices of fine Italian bread, toasted to golden brown, with an outstandingly buttery taste. Yet another family favorite, Focaccia are handmade, crusty flat-bread biscuits that are gently flavored with extra virgin olive oil, herbs, and poppy seeds. And the DiCamillo cookie assortments are virtually staggering in their luscious variety!

All DiCamillo biscotti come handsomely packaged in nine-ounce paper and cellophane bags with ribbon or in extremely tasteful one-pound, two-ounce illustrated canisters. They range in price from $4.00 to $24.00 and can also be found in Bloomingdale's, Macy's, and Neiman-Marcus.

Conveniences: G, P, H, D **Credit Cards:** AE, MC, V **Shipping:** U.S.—X, UPS; A&H—X, UPS; C—R, UPS

Dimpflmeier Bakery

Dimpflmeier Bakery

EXPORT DIVISION
P.O. Box 192, Port Credit, Ontario, L5G4L7 Canada

416·239·3031

*H*old one of these weighty loaves in your hands, look over its dark gnarled crust, close your eyes, and smell the thick rye aroma: You'll swear you could be in one of Munich's old stone-oven bakeries, elbow-to-elbow with a bevy of black-clad hausfraus. That's how good this bread is.

All the credit for this authentic Bavarian specialty goes to Alfons Dimpflmeier, a native Münchener who received his Baker's Diploma from the Handelskammer there before immigrating to Ontario, Canada, in 1957. Dimpflmeier's longing for genuine rye bread from the old country motivated him to bake his own, first for himself and his German friends, then for the Canadians, who quickly recognized a great find.

Dimpflmeier's bakery makes sixteen different varieties of German bread, each with its own special character. Perhaps the most impressive loaf, especially as a gift, is the ten-pound Holzofen Brot. This delicious mild sourdough giant won't fit in your breadbox, but you can slice it into chunks and freeze it without any loss of quality. Fresh, it lasts up to three weeks. It sells for $16.00. You may also order a minimum of four three-pound Holzofen loaves, sliced or unsliced, for $4.30 each. Dimpflmeier's Pumpernickel is world-class and costs $2.10 per one-pound loaf, with a five loaf minimum order. A ten-pound, ten-loaf gift pack of assorted bestsellers is also available.

Conveniences: G, P **Credit Cards:** none **Shipping:** U.S.—UPS; C—UPS

DiCamillo Bakery

NORTHERN LAKES WILD RICE COMPANY
Nutty Wild Rice Bread (unyeasted)

½ stick margarine, softened
¼ cup honey
2 eggs
1⅓ cup cooked Wild Rice
½ cup chopped pecans (or any other nut)
1¼ cup whole wheat flour
1 teaspoon baking powder
1 teaspoon salt
½ teaspoon cloves
½ teaspoon mace
¾ cup milk

Preheat oven to 325°F. Cream margarine and honey. Beat in eggs until smooth. Stir in Wild Rice and nuts. Mix dry ingredients together and stir into egg/rice mixture, alternating one-third at a time with milk. Mix until just combined. Pour into well-greased 8 x 3 x 2½-inch loaf pan. Bake 1 hour, cool on rack 10 minutes, remove from pan, and cool completely. Makes 1 loaf.

Gaston Dupre, Inc.

6201 Johns Road #11, Tampa, Florida 33614
813·885·9445

*P*asta is simple. But, as with many simple foods, the best pasta is made by an involved process that takes time, an ingredient most pasta makers can't allow. Whereas other pastas are "extruded"—a fast process in which the dough is force-fed through a die—Gaston Dupre's pasta is laminated (rolled) according to the time-honored method used in the best Italian neighborhood pasta shops. The dough is hand-folded and fed many times into a set of heavy steel rollers. This labor-intensive procedure allows the gluten in the pasta to rest, which is essential to achieving the proper texture and the quintessential pasta character.

Gaston Dupre uses only the finest hard durum wheat flour and semolina, grown in America's northern plains. And they use eggs rather than water to wet their pasta dough, making it rich and firm. All their pastas have four eggs a pound—thirty percent more than the next-highest in the pasta industry. These and other factors combine to make Gaston Dupre's pasta probably America's best.

The pasta is available in several vibrant, all-natural colors, including Golden Egg, Spinach, Tomato, Beet, Whole Wheat, and Confetti, which is a mixture of all. The pasta is attractively packaged in twelve-ounce boxes for $3.25 each or six bags (any combination) for $19.50, plus $2.75 shipping. Also available at Macy's, Marshall Fields, and Jordan Marsh.

Conveniences: G, H, D **Credit Cards:** AE, MC **Shipping:** U.S.—UPS

Northern Lakes Wild Rice Company

TONY CENICOLA

The Vermont Country Store

Northern Lakes Wild Rice Company

P.O. Box 28, Cass Lake, Minnesota 56633 *(June to November)*

218·335·6369

P.O. Box 392, Teton Village, Wyoming 83025 *(December to May)*

307·733·7192

*E*rnest Nels Anderson takes great pride in explaining that his wild rice is hand-harvested wild rice, not machine-harvested paddy wild rice. "Top quality wild rice should *not* be black and shiny," writes Mr. Anderson, "but dark brown in color, like ours. This assures you the best taste, texture, cooking quality, and maximum yield." Indeed, Florence Fabricant, in an article for the *New York Times,* supports Mr. Anderson's claims: the hand-harvested rice takes half as long to cook and yields more grain than the paddy rice, thus making the *wild* wild rice more economical.

The nutty flavored kernels can be prepared in a variety of ways. You can simply add a pat of butter and a squeeze of lemon juice to the rice, which is actually an aquatic grass, or you can order the company's recipe booklet ($.75) and try your hand at Wild Rice Yeasted Bread, Sherried Wild Rice Soup, Bimiteigun (Chippewa Meat Loaf), Oyster Stuffing, or Wildest Rice Cake, among others.

A one-pound bag sells for $5.70 per pound; the five- and ten-pound bags are $5.50 per pound, plus $2.00 shipping for the first pound and $.40 for every additional pound.

Conveniences: G, P, R **Credit Cards:** none **Shipping:** U.S.—UPS or motor freight; A&H—UPS; C—UPS

The Vermont Country Store

Weston, Vermont 05161

802·463·3855

A small booklet by Vrest Orton relates *The History of and Uses for Vermont Common Crackers®.* It alone is worth the price of the crackers. (But the crackers are good, too!) In 1828, Timothy and Charles Cross first made the crackers in Montpelier. Vermont families at that time usually bought a barrel of 1,200 crackers. Yet the cracker barrel was not so much a symbol of the home as of the country store, says Orton, who quotes Weston Cate, the director of the Vermont Historical Society: "The cracker barrel added a term to the language and became synonymous with informal discussions and idle talk."

These crunchy puffs, which resemble large oyster crackers (but are better) can be eaten plain, with jam or butter, or with pâté or cheese. Most aficionados recommend toasting them under the broiler with a dab of butter. History lends a variation: Try soaking them in ice water for a few minutes, add butter, and place in a hot oven. The crackers make great crumbs for cooking and baking, too. Recipes for Mock Mince Pie, Oyster Stuffing, Country Brunch Casserole, and more are included.

You can order the crackers from Norm Thompson or from the store. The Vermont prices, which are a little lower than others, run $9.95 for a twenty-eight-ounce tin and $1.99 each for a twelve-ounce bag or a ten-ounce box.

Conveniences: P, R **Credit Cards:** MC, V **Shipping:** U.S.—UPS; A&H—UPS; C—UPS

Wolferman's

1900 West 47th Place, Suite 218, Westwood, Kansas 66205

913·432·6131 or 1·800·255·0169

*A*ttention English muffin maniacs! If in your quest for the ultimate English muffin you have not discovered those produced by this ninety-eight-year-old Kansas City, Kansas, company, you shall henceforth remember this day. Just one look at these plump, crispy marvels, and you can almost taste the greatness of what you've been missing. We have doubts you could find a better English muffin even in England!

Louis Wolferman started the company in 1888, and it has remained a family enterprise through four generations, now with Fred Wolferman at the helm. Originally it was a grocery store in downtown Kansas City, but eventually the family's baking talents came to the fore. In the early part of this century, Wolferman's perfected their English muffin recipe, and demand proved so great that all other concerns became secondary.

Wolferman's Original English Muffin is a supreme breakfast experience all by itself, but its variety of other uses is nearly endless: mini pizzas, burgers, eggs Benedict, etc. A case of four-dozen muffins is $17.00, plus $3.90 shipping. A half-case is $10.00, plus $2.90. Wolferman's also makes a Light Wheat Muffin that's excellent (same prices), a Cheddar Cheese Muffin made with real Wisconsin cheddar ($13.00 per half-case), a Cinnamon-Raisin Muffin packed with fat juicy raisins (same price as cheddar), and a Blueberry Muffin made with whole fresh blueberries (also $13.00 per half-case). Wolferman's specializes in fine mail-order gift packages. For example, the company's Five-Way Sampler Case has all the above muffins, four dozen in all, for $20.00, plus $3.90 shipping. They have other fine combinations with jams, teas, honey, hollandaise mixes, and more. Send for their beautiful catalog, or order toll-free by phone.

Conveniences: G, H, R, P, D **Credit Cards:** AE, DC, MC, V, Wolferman's **Shipping:** U.S.—UPS; A&H—X

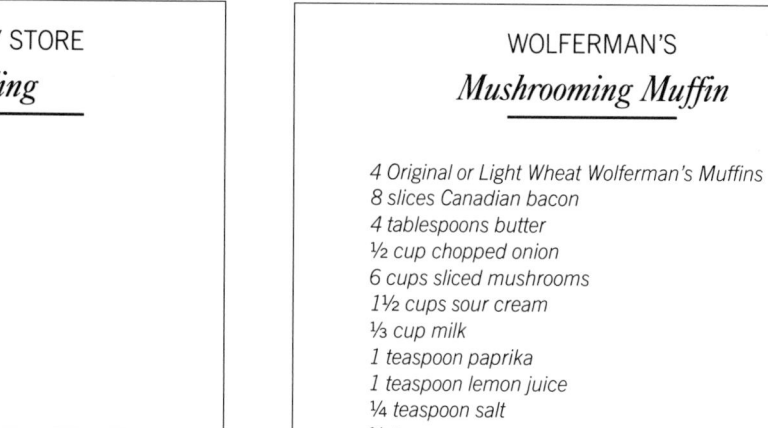

VERMONT COUNTRY STORE
Cracker Pudding

2 eggs, separated
1 cup sugar
Grated rind of 1 lemon
2 tablespoons butter, melted
1 teaspoon vanilla
½ cup coconut
⅓ cup raisins
1 quart milk
3 cups cracker crumbs
⅓ cup jelly
½ cup powdered sugar

Preheat oven to 350°F. Mix together egg yolks and next 8 ingredients. Pour into a buttered 3-quart casserole and bake 1 hour. Spread top with jelly. Beat egg whites till soft peaks form and add powdered sugar, beating till glossy. Spread meringue on top and bake until delicately brown.

WOLFERMAN'S
Mushrooming Muffin

4 Original or Light Wheat Wolferman's Muffins
8 slices Canadian bacon
4 tablespoons butter
½ cup chopped onion
6 cups sliced mushrooms
1½ cups sour cream
⅓ cup milk
1 teaspoon paprika
1 teaspoon lemon juice
¼ teaspoon salt
⅛ teaspoon pepper

Split, toast, and butter English muffins. Brown the Canadian bacon in the butter. Remove from the skillet and keep warm while sautéing the onion in the skillet drippings. Add the mushrooms and simmer until tender. Stir in the sour cream, milk, paprika, lemon juice, salt, and pepper. Heat through. Top muffin halves with bacon slices and spoon on mushroom sauce.

BRIAN LEATART

CHAPTER FIFTEEN

*Soups, Stews
and Prepared Foods*

Bess' Beans

P.O. Box 1542, Charleston, South Carolina 29402

803·722·4559

"*B*eans are Big," says Bess Anderson, owner of Bess' Beans in Charleston, South Carolina, and who could disagree? Start with a colorful bag of Bess' high-quality beans, follow Bess' original Low-Country recipe, and you've got a sumptuous southern-tradition bean soup that will make a believer out of anybody.

Bess began her bean-bagging company less than two years ago, in 1984, and already she's got a booming mail-order business, as well as a burgeoning clientele at her Charleston bean shop. She is especially proud of her traditional Low Country 13-Bean Super Soup, the recipe for which took her four months and many batches to perfect. Bess also sells a soup she calls Triple Pea Plus One, which includes three kinds of peas plus lentils, as well as her own hearty version of Black Bean Soup. All three of Bess' bagged-bean soup bases come with Bess' own recipes. They're ideal for picnics, barbecues, or as starters for fancier country-style dinners.

Bess' 13-Bean Super Soup comes in twelve-ounce bags tied with decorative ribbon for $3.00, or a twenty-four-ounce size for $5.00. Triple Pea Plus One and Black Bean soups come in one-pound bags for $3.00. Shipping is extra, depending on destination and weight, but there's no minimum order.

Conveniences: G, R **Credit Cards:** none **Shipping:** U.S.—R, UPS; A&H—R; C—R

Bess' Beans

Bon Mélange, Inc.

Bon Mélange, Inc.

115 Davis Avenue, Pass Christian, Mississippi 39571

601·452·3258

*F*rom the kitchens of the past to the present, recipes of bone-strengthening, muscle-firming (or so our grandmas would have liked us to believe) hearty soups survive and flourish. Enterprising Malee Hearin began packaging her dried soups for friends and voilá, a business was born. These are truly "the gifts you'll want to give yourself."

The French Market Soup, from New Orleans, is a meal in itself, a medley of eighteen varieties of beans, peas, and barley, plus a hand-tied bag of bouquet garni. Bayou Black Bean Soup, one of our favorites, doubles as an interestingly spicy dip for nachos. The last of Ms. Hearin's tureen trio is a Baton Rouge Bean Soup. "Just add ham hock and simmer," she says. But don't forget the water!

The soups sell for $4.95, plus $2.50 an order. If you're planning for the Christmas season, allow two weeks lead time. You can also order Bon Mélange products through the catalogs of Creole Delicacies, Gazin Robinson, and Way Down Yonder, all of New Orleans. (See pages 104 and 115 for other Bon Mélange items.)

Conveniences: D, G, H, P, R **Credit Cards:** MC, V, ($10.00) **Shipping:** U.S.—UPS; A&H—R, UPS; C—UPS

Casa DiLisio

486 Lexington Avenue, Mt. Kisco, New York 10549

914·666·5021

*D*on't let the name—or the taste—fool you. Casa DiLisio comes from Mt. Kisco, New York, not Italy. These frozen gourmet sauces—Walnut Pesto, Pesto alla Genovese, Sauce Provencal (scampi sauce), and White Clam Sauce—cook up in minutes with delicious results. The European-style aromas that will rise from your kitchen in an American time frame will be sure to please all but the most finicky cooks. The first three sauces can be kept frozen for nine months; the clam sauce, for three to four months. But even buying the minimum order of twelve seven-ounce packages, you'll use up these kitchen helpers in no time at all.

Lucy DiLisio's enclosed recipe brochure lists simple, time-saving ideas for combining her family's sauces with classic foods and dishes: chicken, veal, eggs, potato salad, pasta, even softshell crab. These easy-to-use sauces just beg for experimentation.

The $36.00 price does not include cost of shipping, which depends on the destination. Also, some gourmet stores carry the sauces. Once you've tried the Casa DiLisio line, you may even want to place an order for their half-gallon-size containers.

Conveniences: D, P, R **Credit Cards:** none **Shipping:** U.S.—UPS; A&H—UPS; C—UPS

CASA DILISIO
Pesto Pizza

*F*or a great different pizza, replace tomato sauce with pesto sauce and do everything else the same. Pesto sauce is also great on English muffin pizza. English muffin pizza can be cut into quarters after cooked and served as hot hors d'oeuvres. For a white pizza use walnut sauce instead of tomato and garnish with pepperoni or other combinations.

CASA DILISIO
Shrimp Scampi

*O*ne container of scampi sauce is enough for 1 pound raw, cleaned, deveined shrimp. Heat sauce in saucepan. Wipe shrimp dry. Put raw shrimp in heated sauce. Stir 2–3 minutes. Serve at once with sliced Italian or french bread. Also may be served as hot hors d'oeuvre in chafing dish.

Casa DiLisio

Casa DiLisio

Casa DiLisio

Fresca Gusta

725 West 18th Street, Chicago, Illinois 60616

312·733·0114

JoAnna Simkus' Fresca Gusta sauces grew from her home-tended basil plants, so to speak. Rave reviews of her pesto from family and friends led this Radcliffe graduate to develop nine high-quality frozen sauces: Pesto, White Clam, Bouillabaisse, Rouille (garlic), Sorrel, Black Bean, and the classic White, Brown, and Red.

"With a full complement in the freezer, you're pretty well set for easy elegance," and with Fresca Gusta's cookbook—enclosed with each order—you won't be lacking for ideas. From a sophisticated Grits Riviera to Chicken Kiev to Mushroom and Sorrel Tart, the recipes are organized by type of sauce for easy reference.

The sauces, beautifully packaged with elegant artwork by John Rummelhoff, are available in major department stores such as Macy's, Marshall Field, and Frederick and Nelson. By mail, these gourmet basics come twelve to a case (minimum order is one case) for $25.50. Delivery charge is C.O.D., and no credit cards are accepted. The orders are shipped in insulated boxes with reusable blue ice.

Conveniences: D, P, R **Credit Cards:** none **Shipping:** U.S.—UPS; A&H—Federal Express; C—Federal Express

---

FRESCA GUSTA
Mushroom and Sorrel Tart

½ pound fresh chanterelle mushrooms
½ pound large white mushrooms
3 tablespoons butter
1 jar Fresca Gusta Sorrel Sauce Base
2 tablespoons heavy cream
7-inch x 11-inch (or approximate) unfilled tart shell with
*   pastry strips for lattice topping*
1 egg

Slice mushrooms into ¼-inch slices. (If fresh chanterelles are unavailable, substitute an additional ¾ pound large white mushrooms.) Sauté mushrooms in butter until soft—about 2 minutes. Add Fresca Gusta Sorrel Sauce Base and continue cooking for 3–4 minutes. With slotted spoon, transfer mushrooms into tart shell. Reduce remaining liquid over medium-high heat until thick—about 1 minute. Remove from heat, add cream, mix thoroughly, and pour over mushrooms in tart shell. Top mushrooms with pastry strips in crisscross fashion. Beat egg with a few drops of water and brush on lattice top to glaze. Bake in preheated 375°F oven for 40–45 minutes until crust is golden. Let cool to room temperature and cut into 2-inch squares.

FRESCA GUSTA
East-West Meatballs

1½ pounds ground chuck
1 cup soft bread crumbs
1 egg
1 teaspoon French-style mustard
1 cup red wine
1 jar Fresca Gusta Black Bean Sauce Base
2 tablespoons sour cream

Mix chuck, bread crumbs, egg, and mustard and refrigerate at least 1 hour. Form into meatballs and brown in a saucepan with a bit of olive oil. Drain excess oil from pan. Add Fresca Gusta Black Bean Base and red wine. Simmer for 20 minutes. Remove from heat and stir in sour cream. Serve over noodles or with toothpicks as appetizers.

BRIAN LEATART

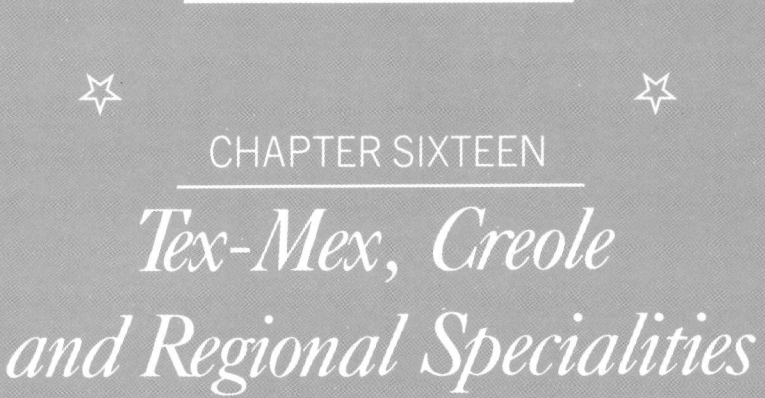

CHAPTER SIXTEEN

*Tex-Mex, Creole
and Regional Specialities*

American Spoon Foods

411 East Lake Street, Petoskey, Michigan 49770

616·347·9030

*A*s a child on vacation with his family in northern Michigan, Justin Rashid foraged through the forests for wild morel mushrooms. Now he forages for a living. Rashid's American Spoon Foods, established in 1979, is one of the only, if not *the* only source in America of dried wild morel mushrooms, that rare springtime delicacy that most people believe can be found only in France. Each year since 1983, American Spoon Foods ships more than two thousand pounds of the gourmet fungi to restaurants and individuals as far away as Hong Kong.

Morels can be used in an endless variety of fine-food combinations, and with each shipment Rashid encloses an array of recipes based on the innovations of his friend, master chef Lawrence Forgione, owner of New York City's An American Place restaurant and pioneer of The New American Cuisine.

One ounce of Dried Morels is $12.50 delivered, with an additional charge for Alaska and Hawaii. All shipments come packaged in attractive wood straw, and gift cards are available on request.

Conveniences: G, R, P **Credit Cards:** MC, V, ($10.00) **Shipping:** U.S.—R, UPS; A&H—R, UPS

American Spoon Foods

THE EL PASO CHILE COMPANY
Salsa de Chile Colorado
(Basic Red Chile Sauce)

---

12 dried medium-length red chile pods
3 cups water
½ teaspoon comino (cumin)
1 tablespoon flour
1 teaspoon salt
1 teaspoon vinegar
½ teaspoon brown sugar
½ teaspoon onion powder
¼ teaspoon garlic powder

Wash chile pods. Remove stems and seeds. Bring chile pods and water to boil. Boil 10 minutes, covered. Remove from heat, cover and let sit 10 more minutes. Pour water and chiles into blender and liquify. Strain sauce through a colander or large sieve. If chile mixture is too thick to pass through colander, thin with water. Return to saucepan. Add water to make 2½ to 3 cups, if necessary. Add remaining ingredients and simmer until thick. Sauce is better when refrigerated for 24 hours.

Bon Mélange, Inc.

115 Davis Avenue, Pass Christian, Mississippi 39571

601·452·3258

*W*hen it comes to sauces, the real cooks separate from the amateurs as distinctly as a yolk from an egg white. To package a sauce and succeed deserves reward which is exactly what these Bon Mélange sauces have. The Rockefeller Sauce mixes up in a snap for the traditional New Orleans treat, Oysters Rockefeller, or for any number of other recipes. Just as versatile is the Cajun Beginnings mix, a "magic package" that transforms ordinary groceries into extraordinarily good jambalaya, etouffee, even gazpacho. The Bienville Sauce can also turn meat and seafood into Creole French delights. Recipes accompany this mushroom cheese sauce as well as the other two sauce mixes.
If you're planning a Creole dinner, you may also want to try Bon Mélange's mix for cheese balls—Onion-Dill, Garlic-Herb, and Curry.
The Say "Cheese," C'est Boursin package sells for $5.95, the sauces for $5.75.
These and other Bon Mélange products (see pages 104 and 111 for more information) make for simple presents, already wrapped and ready to go.

Conveniences: D, G, H, P, R **Credit Cards:** MC, V, ($10.00) **Shipping:** U.S.—UPS; A&H—R, UPS; C—UPS

The El Paso Chile Company™

100 Ruhlin Court, El Paso, Texas 79922

915·544·3434

*A*rtfully packaged with terra-cotta-colored and ristra-red labels, El Paso's Tex-Mex products make perfect presents for hot-blooded friends. Stock your shelves with such basics as Chile Sandias, sun-dried chile pods (one-pound bag for $5.00); Whole Green Chiles Packed in Water ($2.50 a can); and Chile Beans, a pound of pinto beans with special seasonings ($5.00 a bag). Also try the sixteen-ounce jars of Chile Con Queso ($6.50) and Salsa Primera™ ($4.50). The latter's unique tang comes from a blend of natural ingredients: tomatoes, green chiles, onions, and cilantro—with no added salt.
The company, founded in 1981 by a mother-and-son team, also offers three especially attractive gift assortments: a twig basket ($50.00), an earth-tone bag ($29.00), and a Mexican clay pot shaped like a goat ($50.00); all include a wealth of recipes. Write directly to the company or order through Neiman-Marcus, Macy's, Marshall Fields, or Williams-Sonoma. Speigel, Horchow, and Trifles also carry El Paso products (see page 54 for wreaths). Delivery charges are extra.

Conveniences: G, P, R **Credit Cards:** MC, V **Shipping:** U.S.—R, X, UPS; A&H—R; C—R, X, UPS

Market Square Food Company

1642 Richfield, Highland Park, Illinois 60035

312·831·2228 *or* **1·800·232·2299**

*T*his smart, well-respected Illinois company has taken a particularly sensitive view of the new American movement toward gourmet food, and especially of this country's great potential in the area.
"It is time," reads the company's catalog, "to realize that within the scope of international foods and their preparation, Americans need not be so humble. Within our own boundaries lie the finest produce created by nature for the partaking of man." Market Square Food makes a business of just this—collecting certain of America's finest foods, and making them available for our happy partaking.
One such collectible is Market Square's Extra Fancy Long Grain Wild Rice, from the northern lakes of Minnesota. This rare delicacy has become a treasured commodity worldwide. Its rich, deep flavor simply cannot be equaled by other rices. And, as in centuries past, today the long dark grains are still harvested by American Indians in canoes.
Market Square Food Company offers their fancy rice in a handsomely illustrated one-pound tin for $15.00, in a twelve-ounce polished tan paper bag for $8.50, or in a functional sixteen-ounce vacuum-packed polybag for $10.00. The products are also widely available in department stores such as Bloomingdale's, B. Altman, Macy's, and Marshall Fields.

Conveniences: D, G, R **Credit Cards:** MC, V, ($15.00) **Shipping:** U.S.—UPS; A&H—UPS; C—UPS

Market Square Food Company

Desert Rose Salsa Company Inc.

Desert Rose Salsa Company Inc.

P.O. Box 5391, Tucson, Arizona 85703

602·743·0450

*I*n a great majority of the North American continent, it is virtually impossible to find good Mexican food, either as a prepared dish or as the necessary ingredients to prepare it yourself. Yes, the problem was a profound one, but the solution is now upon us, in the delightful form of Desert Rose Homemade Salsa. This is unquestionably one of the best, richest, fullest salsas obtainable in the country.

Steve and Patti Swidler started the company in 1977, working out of their Tucson, Arizona, home. As their company has grown they have maintained the highest-quality ingredients in their salsa, such as the finest tomatoes, jalapeño peppers, onions, carrots, herbs, and spices. All of their natural salsas are prepared without water, sugar, artificial preservatives, or flavorings.

Desert Rose Salsa is available in three degrees of picante: Medium, Hot, and Conmemorativa. This last is their special gold-label edition, made from a blend of medium salsa, green salsa, and a rare Mexican pepper available only seasonally.

Desert Rose also makes a great Salsa Enchilada and a rich mélange of mildly hot cherry peppers in spiced olive oil called Alberta's Peppers. Desert Rose Salsa offers a three-jar (sixteen ounces each) gift pack of their salsas for $13.75, plus shipping. Or there's a six-jar gift pack which includes two jars of Alberta's Peppers for $26.50, plus shipping. Salsa is also available by the case.

Conveniences: G, R, P, H, D **Credit Cards:** none **Shipping:** U.S.—UPS; A&H—R; C—R

Genovesi Food Company

P.O. Box 5668, Dayton, Ohio 45405

513·277·2173

Genovesi's simply packed Dried Tomatoes in a jar are deceiving. Opening the red top is the first step to a richly but not overwhelmingly spiced fruit treat. Yes, fruit. These dried tomatoes will remind you of the love apple's traditional category, for you'll taste the very subtle sweetness that is so perfectly complemented by the garlic, oregano, and salt. Packed in sunflower or olive oil, the tomatoes blend exquisitely with garden pasta salads, soft cheeses, shellfish, and chicken.

If you've never tried a dried tomato, try these. If you've tried a dried tomato and didn't like it, try Genovesi. They just may turn your taste buds around.

Thank Nicole Genovesi for cultivating this much-loved Italian specialty in America's heartland. Although her family had been producing the tomatoes for fifteen years, it wasn't until 1983 that Nicole increased production and began to offer these Midwestern treats nationwide. You can also find the delicacies in the catalogs of American Spoon Foods and Giant Foods.

Three eight-and-a-half-ounce jars of the tomatoes in sunflower oil will cost $21.00, plus $3.00 for shipping and handling. The olive oil three-pack runs for $27.00, plus $3.00.

Conveniences: D, P, R **Credit Cards:** none **Shipping:** U.S.—UPS; A&H—UPS; C—UPS

GENOVESI FOOD COMPANY
Grilled Goat Cheese

---

1 (8 ounces) jar grape leaves
1 cup Genovesi Dried Tomatoes
4 ounces Montrachet goat cheese, cut in ¼-inch slices

Carefully remove grape leaves from the jar, rinse, and pat dry. Lay leaves out on a flat work surface. Place a dried tomato in the center of a grape leaf, lay slice of goat cheese over the tomato and top with another dried tomato. Bring leaf up around tomatoes and cheese, folding so that there is no cheese or tomato exposed. Proceed in this manner until all goat cheese and tomatoes have been used.

Place leaves on a grill over hot coals and grill 2–3 minutes on each side. Serve immediately.

Makes about 12 hors d'oeuvre.

Genovesi Food Company

House of Tsang

TSANG AND MA
P.O. Box 294, Belmont, California 94002
415·595·2270

*H*ere's an easy way to make fine Oriental food at home, without the hassle of scouring Chinatowns or specialty shops for the right ingredients. House of Tsang, a young company based near San Francisco, offers a line of seven Oriental cooking and table sauces and dressings that will turn you into a master chef and a devotee of Oriental home-cooking. Electrical engineers David Tsang and William Sher started the company with Dennis Ma in 1975. Recognizing the gap in America's Oriental food market at the gourmet level, the partnership began by importing Oriental vegetable seeds, mainly from The People's Republic of China. They still sell the imported seeds—of such impossible-to-find vegetables as dow gauk, mao gwa, yuen sai, and siew choy—but have since expanded to fine Oriental sauces. Their line now includes light, dark, mushroom, and ginger-flavored Soy Sauces, Mandarin Marinade, Teriyaki Sauce, Szechuan Hot and Sour Dressing, Hong Kong Barbecue Sauce, and Sweet and Sour Concentrate. Flavored oils include Hot and Spicy Mongolian Fire, Hot Chili Sesame, Singapore Curry Oil, and garlic- and ginger-flavored Wok Oil. Prices range from $3.00 to $4.00 per ten-ounce bottle.

Conveniences: R, P, D **Credit Cards:** MC, V **Shipping:** U.S.—UPS; A&H—R, UPS; C—R, UPS

Vieux Carré Foods Inc.

P.O. Box 26956, New Orleans, Louisiana 70186
504·525·3880

*V*ieux Carré Foods probably has the most complete line of authentic Creole sauces anywhere. At the top of their list is a relatively new product they call Hurricane Mix, which is a spicy hot sauce with plenty of jolt, yet with a deep Cajun character all its own. It comes in twelve-ounce jars that sell for $4.25 each, with a three-jar minimum. More traditional is their Shrimp Remoulade Sauce, which turns shrimp and other seafoods into regional gourmet specialties. Use it hot, or cold as with a shrimp cocktail. It comes in nine-ounce jars at $3.50 each, three-jar minimum. Some other products from their fine line include: Creole Mustard, New Orleans Seafood Sauce, Louisiana Hot Sauce, Gumbo File, Creole Praline Sauce, and Old Fashioned Roux. They all have origins in the gourmet specialties of the region and are of the highest quality available.
Vieux Carré features some interesting and delicious gift packs. For example, their Three Jar Pack includes one Creole Praline Sauce, one Creole Mustard, and one New Orleans Seafood Sauce. It sells for $15.00, shipping included.

Conveniences: G, P, R, H, D **Credit Cards:** AE, MC, V **Shipping:** U.S.—UPS; A&H—UPS; C—R, UPS

House of Tsang

Vieux Carré Foods Inc.

Sources

Additional Mail-Order Sources

Ace Pecan Co.
P.O. Box 65, Cordele, GA 31015
800·323·9754
Nut of the Month Plan

Amana Meat Shop and Smokehouse
One Smokehouse Lane, Amana, IA 52203
319·622·3113
Sausage, bacon, etc.

Andrizzi's™ Premium Belgium Waffle Mix
c/o ADC, 1186 Yulupa Avenue, #109,
Santa Rosa, CA 95405
707·579·2595
Belgium waffle mix

Balducci's
424 Avenue of the Americas, New York, NY 10011
800·228·2028, ext. 72, 212·673·2600
Specialty foods

Baldwin Hill Bakery
Baldwin Hill Road, Phillipston, MA 01331
617·249·4691
Sourdough bread

Bon Vivant
36425 Churchill Drive, Solon, OH 44139
216·248·3911
Specialty foods

Brae Beef
The New Butcher Shop, Stamford Town Center,
100 Greyrock Place, Stamford, CT 06901
800·323·4484
Preservative-free beef

Butterfield Farms
330 Washington Street, Marina del Rey, CA 90291
213·822·0700
Fruitcake

Campbell Farms
P.O. Box 74, Post Mills, VT 05058
802·685·3813
Roast suckling pig

Cape Cod™ Potato Chips
Breeds Hill Road, Hyannis, MA 02601
617·775·3206
Potato chips

Cavanaugh Lakeview Farms Ltd.
P.O. Box 430, Chelsea, MI 48118
800·243·4438
Poultry, ham

Caviarteria
29 East 60 Street, New York, NY 10022
800·221·1020, 212·759·7410
Caviar

Chef Allen's Restaurant
The Shoppes at Concorde Centre,
191 Street off Biscayne Boulevard, Miami, FL 33179
800·327·8456, ext. 12, 800·432·2382, ext. 12 (in FL)
Stone crabs

The Chocolate Catalogue
Karl Bissinger French Confections,
3983 Gratiot, St. Louis, MO 63110
800·325·8881
Truffles, novelty chocolates, etc.

Collin Street Bakery
408 West Seventh Avenue, Corsicana, TX 75110
214·872·8111
Fruitcake

Community Kitchens™
P.O. Box 3778, Baton Rouge, LA 70821-3778
800·535·9901, 504·381·3900
Coffee, tea, preserves, dressings, etc.

Conrad Rice Mill
P.O. Box 296, New Iberia, LA 70560
318·364·7242
Rice

Country Estate Pecans
L & C Gourmet Products, Inc.,
P.O. Box 12607, Tuscon, AZ 85732
602·791·2062
Pecans

Crinklaw Farms
P.O. Box 706, King City, CA 93930
408·385·3261, 408·385·6658
Elephant garlic, chiles, bay leaf wreaths

Cryer Creek Kitchens
Box 1029, Corsicana, TX 75110
800·468·0088
Cheesecake, chocolates, nuts, etc.

Czimer Foods
Route 7, Box 285, Lockport, IL 60441
312·460·2210
Game

D'Artagnan, Inc.
399 St. Paul Avenue, Jersey City, NJ 07306
201·792·0748
American foie gras, smoked duck

Dean & DeLuca
Mail-order Dept., 110 Greene Street,
Suite 304, New York, NY 10012
800·221·7714, 212·431·1691
Specialty foods

Downeast Seafood Express
Box 138, Brooksville, ME 04617
800·556·2326
Fresh lobster

Durey-Libby
P.O. Box 345, Carlstadt, NJ 07072
201·939·2775
Nuts

Eagle Rice & Feed Mills, Inc.
P.O. Box 268, Crowley, LA 70527-0268
318·783·0881
Rice

Exotic Foods International
236 North Hayes Street,
P.O. Box 760, Bellefontaine, OH 43311
513·599·3319
Canned game foods

Fabrique Delices
41 South Railroad Avenue, San Mateo, CA 94401
415·344·5769
Pate

Farms of Texas Company
P.O. Box 1305, Alvin, TX 77512
713·331·6481
Rice

Fiesta Nut Corp.
P.O. Box 366, 75 Harbor Road, Port Washington, NY 11050
800·645·3296, 516·883·1403
Nuts, chocolate-covered nuts

Figi's
Dairy Lane, Marshfield, WI 54404
**715·384·6101 (to place an order),
715·387·6311 (to inquire about an order)**
Cheese, smoked meats, preserves, cookies, etc.

The Forst's
CPO Box 1000P,
12-24 Ten Broeck Avenue, Kingston, NY 12401
800·453·4010, 914·331·3500
Game birds, beef, poultry, ham

Foxhill
Box 7, Parma, MI 49269
517·531·3179
Herbs

Gérard Haut Cuisine
Main Street, Fairfax, VT 05454
802·849·6141
Duck liver

Ghossain Mid East Bakery
2935 Market Street, Youngstown, OH 44507
216·782·9473
Pita, flatbread

Glen Echo Farms
Box 21B, Wendell, NH 03783
603·863·6780
Spring lamb

Goodies from Goodman
12102 Inwood Road, Dallas, TX 75234
214·387·4804
Candy

Gordon-Thompson, Ltd.
410 West Coast Highway, Newport Beach, CA 92663
714·645·5180
Wild game and exotic foods

Gourmet Nut Center
1430 Railroad Avenue, Orland, CA 95963
916·865·5511
Almonds, pistachios, candy-coated nuts

Grandma Morgan's Gourmet Kitchen
P.O. Box 972, Lake Oswego, OR 97034
503·761·4303
Specialty foods

Green River Trout Farm
R.R. 1, Box 267, Mancelona, MI 49659
800·632·9616, 616·584·3486
Smoked fish, poultry, buffalo sausage, morels

Harrington's
170B-5 Main Street, Richmond, VT 05477
802·434·4444
Meats, poultry, cheese

Harry and David
Bear Creek Orchards, Medford, OR 97501
503·776·2400
Fruit of the Month, smoked meats, cookies, etc.

Hawaiian Plantations
1311 Kalakaua Avenue, Honolulu, HI 96826
800·367·2177, 808·955·8888
Pineapples, chocolate-covered macademias, stuffed dates, jams, jellies, etc.

Herbs Now!
The Garden Gourmet, P.O. Box 775, Highland Park, IL 60035
312·432·7711
Herbs

House of Rice
4112 University Way N.E., Seattle, WA 98105
206·633·5181
Basmati rice

Ili Ili Farms
Box 150-B, Kula, HI 96790
800·367·8004
Maui onions, honey, tea, etc.

Jaarsma Bakery
727 Franklin, Pella, IA 50219
515·628·2940
Spiced Christmas cookies, letter cookies

Kohn's Smokehouse
CR 35, Box 160, Thomaston, ME 04861
207·372·8412
Smoked lobster, trout, mussels, salami

Lambs Farm
P.O. Box 520, Libertyville, IL 60048
312·362·4636
Cookies, preserves, cheese, breads

Larch and Jan Hanson
Box 15, Steuben, ME 04680
207·546·2875
Edible seaweed

Lavin's Meats
6428 Union Avenue, Alliance, OH 44601
800·822·0220
Gourmet steaks and hams

Le Gourmet Canadien
988 Elgin Avenue, Winnipeg, Canada R3E 1B4
800·665·0272 , 204·786·1154
Wild rice, maple syrup, caviar, honey, etc.

Lindsay Farms
P.O. Box 581, Atlanta, GA 30361
404·233·2343
Preserves, nuts, candies

Livingston Farms
2224 Livingston Road, Route 3, St. Johns, MI 48879
517·224·3616
Peppermint and spearmint oils, maple syrup

Maple Grove
167 Portland Street, St. Johnsbury, VT 05819
802·748·3136
Maple products, cheese, preserves, etc.

Mariani Nut Company
P.O. Box 664, 709 Dutton Street, Winters, CA 95694
916·795·3311
Almonds, walnuts, pistachios, dried fruits

Maytag Dairy Farm
R.R. 1, Box 806, Newton, IA 50208
800·247·2458, 800·BLU·CHES (in IA), 515·792·1133
Blue cheese, white cheddar cheese, gift boxes

Michael W. Phillips & Co.
P.O. Box 1034, Kennett Square, PA 19348
215·444·3319
Shiitake mushrooms

Mission Orchards
P.O. Box 6387, San Jose, CA 95150
408·297·5056
Specialty foods

Missouri Dandy Pantry
212 Hammons Drive East, Stockton, MO 65785
417·276·5121
Nuts and candies

Neuchatel Chocolates
1369 Avenue of the Americas, New York, NY 10019
212·489·9320
Truffles, Chocolate-of-the-Month Club

Norm Thompson
P.O. Box 3999, Portland, OR 97208
800·547·1160
Smoked salmon

Northwestern Coffee Mills
217 North Broadway, Milwaukee, WI 53202
414·276·1031
Coffee, tea, coffee substitutes, herbs, extracts

Nueske Hillcrest Farm Meats
R.R. 2, Wittenberg, WI 54499
800·382·2266, 800·372·2266 (in WI)
Ham, bacon, sausage, smoked specialty poultry

Nuts D'Vine
P.O. Box 589, Edenton, NC 27932
800·334·0492
Peanuts, peanut butter, oil

Oakwood Game Farm
Box 274, Princeton, MN 55371
800·328·6647, 612·389·2077
Game birds

Omaha Steaks International
P.O. Box 3300, Omaha, NB 68103
800·228·9055, 402·391·3660 (in NB, call collect)
*Hand-trimmed steaks, lamb, veal,
and other frozen gourmet foods*

Paradigm Chocolate Company
5755 SW Jean Road, Lake Oswego, OR 97034
503·636·4880
Chocolate and caramel sauces

Pasta Productions
12358 SW 117 Court, Miami, FL 33186
305·233·3377
Squid ink, citrus, garden vegetable, and chocolate pastas

Peanut Supply Company
114 North Houston, P.O. Box 860, Denison, TX 75020
214·463·3161
Peanuts

Pecos Valley Spice Company
186 Fifth Avenue, New York, NY 10010
212·620·7700
Chiles, tortillas, etc.

Pepperidge Farm Mail Order Co., Inc.
P.O. Box 931, Route 145, Clinton, CT 06413
800·243·9314, 203·669·9245
Soups, cookies, desserts, etc.

Pinnacle Orchards
441 South Fir, Medford, OR 97501
800·547·0227
Fruit

Proper Puddings
912 President Street, Brooklyn, NY 11215
212·783·2486
Plum pudding

Provender
3883 Main Road, Tiverton, RI 02878
401·624·8096
Fine foods

Rathdowney Herbs & Herb Crafts
The Marketplace, Bridgewater, VT 05034
802·672·5116
Herbs

REI
P.O. Box C-88127, Seattle, WA 98188-0127
**800·426·4840, 800·562·4894 (in WA),
206·575·3287 (in Canada and AK)**
Smoked salmon, camping foods

Road Runner Pecans
1985 Salopek Road, Las Cruces, NM 88005
505·526·5949
Pecans

Roy L. Hoffman & Sons
Route 6, Box 5, Hagerstown, MD 21740
301·739·2332
Smoked meats, poultry

Scarlett's Secret English Toffee
Juneau, Inc., P.O. Box 138044, Chicago, IL 60613
312·621·1022
Toffee

S.E. Rykoff & Company
P.O. Box 21467, Los Angeles, CA 90021
213·622·4131
Specialty foods

The Silver Palate
274 Columbus Avenue, New York, NY 10023
800·847·4747
Chutneys, mustards, preserves, vinegars, sauces, etc.

Smithfield Ham & Products Co.
P.O. Box 487, Smithfield, VA 23430
800·628·2242, 804·357·2121
Hams, chili, barbecue, etc.

Southern Rice Marketing
P.O. Box 880, Brinkley, AR 72021
501·734·1233
Rice

Splendid Chocolates Ltd.
Sahagian & Associates, Inc.,
115 North Oak Park Avenue, Oak Park, IL 60301-1303
312·848·5552
Heat-and-serve chocolate fondue

Summerfield Farm
Route 1, Box 43, Boyce, VA 22620
703·837·1718
Veal, beef

Sunnyland Farms
Albany, GA 31703
912·436·5654
Pecans

Surry Shop Peanuts
10208 Ranger Road, Fairfax, VA 22030
703·385·7368
Peanuts

The Swiss Colony
1112 Seventh Avenue, Monroe, WI 53566
214·869·3000
Cheese, meats, candies, etc.

Totem Smokehouse
1906 Pike Place, Seattle, WA 98101
800·9·SALMON
Smoked salmon

Union Stockyards
4538 South Marshfield Avenue, Chicago, IL 60609
800·257·2977, 312·376·7445
Meats

Victorian Pantry, Inc.
P.O. Box 222, Village Station, Saratoga, CA 95071
408·734·0907
Chutneys, preserves, dessert sauces, salad dressings

Wehah Farm, Inc.
P.O. Box 369, Richvale, CA 95974
916·882·4551
Rice

Westnut
P.O. Box 125, Dundee, OR 97115
503·538·2161
Hazelnuts

Willacrik Farm
P.O. Box 599, Templeton, CA 93465
805·238·2776
Elephant garlic

Williams-Sonoma
5750 Hollis Street, Emeryville, CA 94608
415·652·1555
Specialty foods

Wisconsin Fishing Company
P.O. Box 965, Green Bay, WI 54305
414·437·3582
Seafood

Woodland Pantry
Forest Foods, Inc., 138 Wright Lane, Oak Park, IL 60302
312·848·3144
Wild mushrooms

York Harbor Export, Inc.
P.O. Box 737, Varrell Lane, York Harbor, ME 03911
207·363·7206
Belon oysters

Zabar's
2245 Broadway, New York, NY 10024
800·221·3347, 212·787·2000
Specialty foods

Index